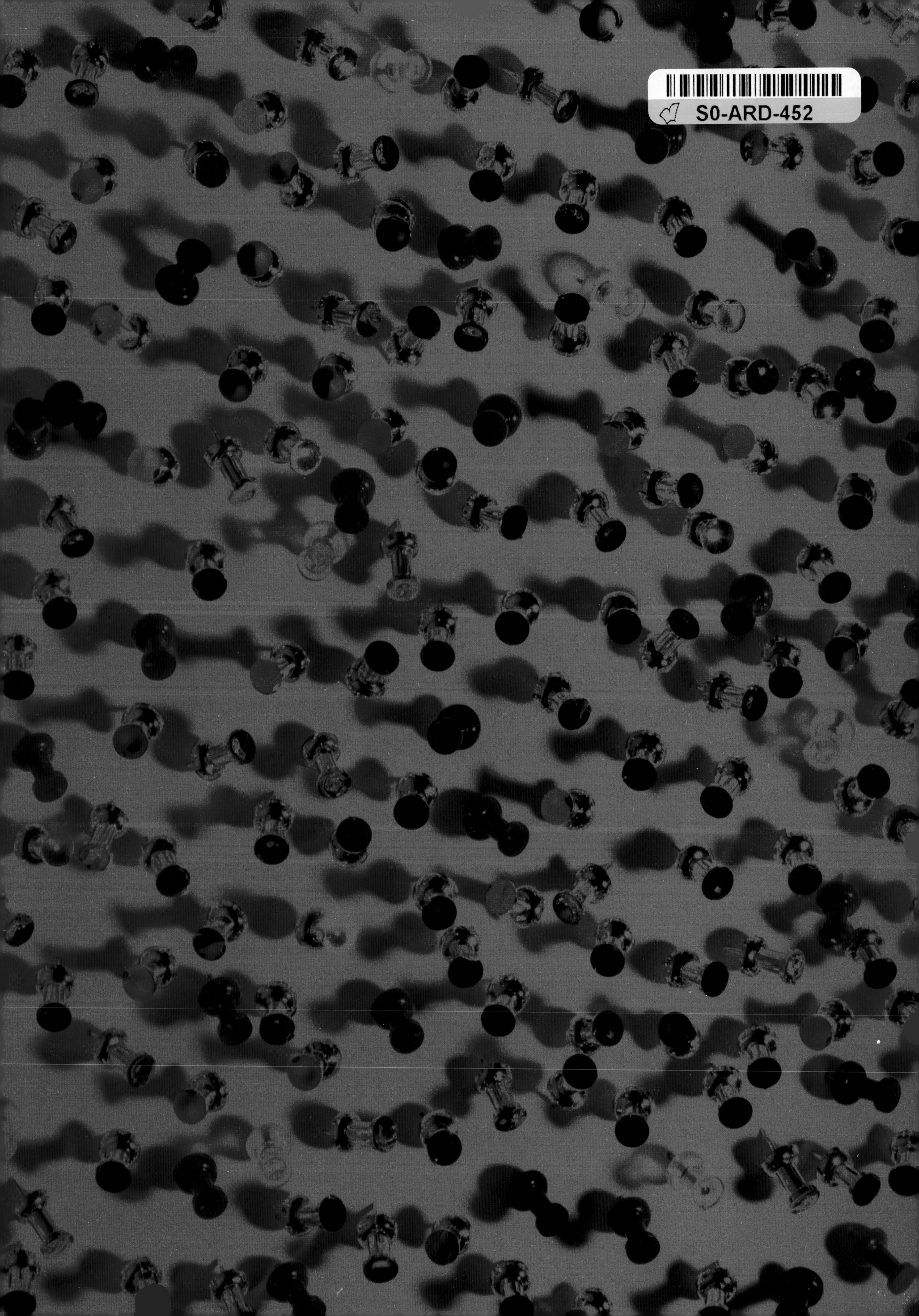
S0-ARD-452

DVERTISING'S TEN BEST OF THE DECADE 1980-1990.

PUBLISHED BY
The One Club for Art and Copy
New York, NY

Mary Warlick
EDITOR

Allan Beaver
DESIGNER

Sheryl Robins
ASSISTANT EDITOR

Ryuichi Minakawa
ART DIRECTOR

Naomi Minakawa
LAYOUT AND PRODUCTION

Cailor/Resnick
(Front, back covers, divider page, end pages)
PHOTOGRAPHER

Commercial On-Line-Systems, Inc.
COMPUTATIONS

Keefe & Associates, Inc.
TYPESETTING

All Union Press, Inc.
POSTSCRIPT™ OUTPUT

Published and distributed by
The One Club for Art & Copy, Inc.
3 West 18th Street
New York, NY 10011

First printing
ISBN 0-929837-02-9

Printed in Japan by Toppan Printing Co.

Board of Directors

EDITOR'S NOTE

At the close of 1989, The One Club asked its executive Board of Directors to name their choices for the top ten ads of the decade. The thirteen board members, belonging to the ranks of the top creative talent in the country, sifted through thousands of award winning advertising for their choices. Their comments, together with their criteria for judging, amounts to the first critical assessment of creative advertising in the '80s.

The list of the top ten ad campaigns of the decade actually resulted in twelve ads due to a three-way tie for ninth. The results were tallied by an independent balloting company. All of the ads nominated for the top ten list are published in the second half of the book. These ads cover the entire spectrum of advertising in the '80s. They range from the classic graphic Volkswagen ad of 1980 to the high energy television commercial, *Bo Diddley*, for Nike released in the summer, 1989.

I would like to thank the many people who contributed to this book, particularly the board members of The One Club, and the creative teams of the winning twelve ads who so generously took time to record their recollections about the germination of the work. Their comments are printed together with the top twelve ads. I owe special thanks to Allan Beaver, who has devoted much time and thought to the design of the book, to Robert Reitzfeld, President of The One Club, who has always had great faith in the project and to Mike Hughes who first suggested the naming of the top ten of the decade early in the Fall, 1989.

Thanks to Sheryl Robins, Clarke Clemens and Wendy Becker who each put in many hours on the project. And thanks to Izabella Piestrzynska, copy editor and to Ryuichi Minakawa who was the art director for the layout and text. Thanks also to Reuven Kopitchinski, photographer, and to the many people in agencies throughout the country who provided the visual material, scripts and other supporting material necessary to see the project's completion.

Advertising's Ten Best of the Decade is the result of a combined effort by all these people, but more importantly, it is the product of higher standards of creativity recognized by The One Show during the past ten years.

Mary Warlick
Director

PRESIDENT'S MESSAGE

1990 A new year, a new decade. And a time to step back and look at what went on in our industry over the past ten years. One thing is for certain, television really came of age in the '80s. And as this book will show, it was advertising's star of the '80s. Spurred on by extremely talented directors and exciting new film techniques, it was sometimes difficult to tell the difference between MTV and the commercials. But a great commercial (or any great ad for that matter) has to start with a great idea. No matter how beautifully produced, a mindless piece of fluff is still a mindless piece of fluff.

So The One Club set out to find the ten best pieces of advertising produced in the past decade. In its Board of Directors it had a built-in panel of judges that would be difficult to top in their talents or their dedication to their professions. This book represents the results of that judging and will surely serve as a valuable reference throughout the '90s.

How good was the advertising in the '80s? Was it better than the '60s? The '70s?

Was Muhammed Ali better than Joe Louis?

Robert Reitzfeld

In advertising, the '60s were funny, the '70s were all business and the '80s were just plain fun. Randy Newman sang about loving L.A., raisins sang about grapevines and Michael Jackson sang with his hair on fire. Wendy's, Frank Perdue and Walter Mondale all wondered where the beef was, and a long line of nervous white-collar nellies, who should have called Federal Express, worried where their packages were. By far the most interesting advertising was created for running shoes, wine coolers and personal computers. Why couldn't the people who need it most— the American automakers— get advertising as good as Nike or Levi's?

In the 1980s advertising stopped being a New York product and started being an American product. Man for man, woman for woman, the advertising people in L.A., San Francisco, Portland, Oregon, Minneapolis and Richmond, Virginia, proved themselves in the 1980s to be at least as good as their New York peers.

Comparisons are often made between the '60s and the '80s. About the time Elvis Presley, Carl Perkins, Chuck Berry and others were creating rock and roll (a new kind of music), the people at Doyle Dane Bernbach were creating a new, human, honest kind of advertising. Nothing that significant happened to music or to advertising in the 1980s. But in advertising, at least, a lot of people got better at their crafts. Never before have there been so many good-looking television commercials. (Most are still pretty stupid; but don't they look nice?)

I used as my criteria for judging the best work of the 1980s the following:

1. The ad makes me believe the product or service being advertised is, in some way, better than its competitors.
2. It's a good, entertaining, interesting salesman.
3. It doesn't insult me. It strikes me as honest and intelligent.
4. I wish I had made it.
5. The advertiser got his money's worth.

Mike Hughes

Selecting the ten best was difficult, indicating that the decade had indeed produced some very exceptional work. It was a decade where many relied on big productions rather than big ideas. However, the advertising that was breakthrough and unique was, for the most part, very entertaining.

It was advertising that was based on humanity and the product's relevance to the consumer.

In retrospect, I believe we can say it was a very productive ten years for the advertising industry.

My criteria for judging singled out those communications which were based on a strategically sound and unique position, which were executed with great craftsmanship and which resulted in an ingenious solution that in some way was breaking new ground in the industry.

Allan Beaver

One obvious development in the '80s has been the proliferation of agencies doing excellent work outside of New York City. Another has been the formation of new agencies, driven by their creative work, that are vying to form the next generation of shops that will become an important voice in the industry. Still another has been the emergence of agencies outside the U.S., notably the U.K., whose work has influenced agencies here.

Yet creatively, all was not well. The bull market that lasted most of the decade failed to produce the climate of receptivity toward good advertising that had characterized the prosperity of the '60s. But as always happens, good work got done anyway. A few campaigns, notably Federal Express, expanded the possibilities of the craft.

As for the selection of the "ten best"— unfortunately, when you're picking only ten pieces from an entire decade, you're judging budgets and media as well as executions. Even though I voted for it, I'm not sure the Wendy's *Where's the Beef?* TV spot is better advertising than some print executions that didn't make it onto my list. Yet the spot (and the phrase) passed into the culture and became a sort of pop icon in ways that advertising seldom does.

As for my criteria for judging, I like advertising that's supported by a big idea and executed in a way that causes me to see the product as though for the first time. And I suppose like everyone else, I apply the envy test: If I wish I'd done it myself, it usually gets a vote.

Tom Thomas

I think the most surprising thing about advertising in the '80s was its range. From the 5,000-word-a-minute Federal Express fast-talking man to the speechless no-frills NYNEX furniture stripper. Music became not a blanket for words but an integral part of the commercial concept. Everyone was out for a new "look" and several found it. From Pytka to Dektor to Godley & Creme. Although I don't like to define a decade in three words or less, I will say that the '80s were a very interesting time to be in advertising.

The thinking behind my choices for the best of the '80s was simple. Was it original? Did it break new ground? Did it start a trend? In other words, was it something everyone else tried to copy and claim credit for the second it appeared.

Helayne Spivak

The majority of the best advertising of the '80s is a direct descendant of the best advertising of the '70s. And the '60s.

Inventive. Surprising. Engaging. Occasionally dramatic. Usually funny. But always communicating a rational reason to buy an advertiser's product.

A beer that tasted great and was less filling. A company that could absolutely, positively deliver overnight.

In the mid-80s, though, a few remarkable commercials made a direct hit on the right brain. They didn't sell with logic, but with attitude.

And they weren't even fashion commercials. They were for products like athletic shoes and computers.

Without claims, without support, sometimes even without words, they made their points loudly and clearly.

In the process, they also brought advertising as close to an art form as it's ever gotten. Do they represent a trend? Probably not.

But they've clearly pushed the envelope of indirection, inference, and faith in a consumer's ability to get an advertising message without being pounded over the head with it.

Hopefully, they've made all of us in advertising aim a little higher.

Diane Rothschild

Overall quality diminished during the decade.

There was much derivative work but little new ground was broken.

There was a healthy broadening of good work being done throughout the country although increasingly there was work done for pro bono or small accounts which won medals.

TV productions' budgets soared.

As for my criteria for judging the ten best:

If they don't see it they don't notice it.

If they don't notice it they don't remember it.

If they don't remember it they don't buy it.

If they don't buy it the agency is fired.

Ron Anderson

No matter what the decade, a great selling concept is a great selling concept. I think the variable lies in the production. In the '80s, the production values soared to new heights enhancing great ideas and sometimes masking mediocre ones. And like all decades, usually one successful campaign spawns several imitators. Almost like spinoffs from a sitcom. Commercials in the latter part of the '80s started to experiment in editing. They became less hindered by logical progression of scenes, while cameras were unlocked and hand-held. Sometimes it worked, sometimes it didn't.

Choosing only ten was difficult. I began by selecting from memory the campaigns in the last ten years that came to mind. Then I went through all the One Show annuals and selected the few remaining ones. My judging criteria consisted of three things: concept, concept, concept.

Anthony Angotti

Advertising in the '80s wasn't as exciting as it was in the '60s but was a lot more exciting than it was in the '70s.

I discovered that those early ads to come out of Minneapolis weren't a freak accident. Thank God (and Tom McElligott).

And fortunately, what happened in Minneapolis didn't just stay in Minneapolis.

I believe the work coming out of there showed art directors and copywriters throughout the country that doing print doesn't have to be a bore. But I must admit I still find it hard to believe that the excitement the industry needed came out of a place like Minneapolis, Minnesota.

I always thought it would come out of Weehawken, New Jersey.

Sal DeVito

I found the judging of the best of the '80s to be like a mini course in recent commercial art history. And I found it really encouraging.

Although every year had its superlative examples, and the final list was fairly evenly spread throughout the decade, the overall quality of the work appeared to get better and better as the years went by. Particularly on the art side. Art directors are doing a much better job with the page today than in the early '80s. And more and more film has taken on a great look.

As I studied the gold, silver and bronze winners over the years, I could see the emergence of the agencies outside of New York: Chiat/Day, Fallon McElligott and McKinney & Silver in particular, influencing print mostly, but also lighting a fire under the whole industry. Toward the latter part of the decade I saw New York respond and more "suburban" agencies taking the lead. And that's not just an opinion, it's reflected in the slate of One Show winners.

Overall I think the whole industry has benefited from a return to creative that characterized the '80s.

Tom Monahan

There was some legitimately great work. But there was less substance than in the '70s. Or the '60s. We came down with a case of the MTVs. Long on flash, short on communication. Mostly, short on thinking. All too often, creatives passed the buck to directors or performers and counted on them to rescue a weak idea with technique. So a lot of work was beautiful, but dumb. I think many agencies were so preoccupied with buying and selling themselves that they became creatively lazy.

I voted for work that moved me without my having to think. It really didn't matter whether it struck my heart, brain, kishkes or alimentary canal. As long as it had that instant clarity that a fresh perception always does. I particularly loved pieces that made me cry. Or jealous as hell.

Tom Nathan

In the 1980s, creative teams, directors and producers watched Spielberg movies and music videos and brought what they saw to the world of commercial production. It was an exciting process to watch and participate in. The downside of it all is that today, an idea, no matter how tenuous, can be dressed up by "good film." If more of us can fuse great ideas and great production, the '90s should be something to behold.

In selecting the best of the '80s, I tried to chose work that was so disturbingly good, copywriters and art directors coming afterwards could not avoid being influenced by it.

Larry Cadman

By and large, I chose work that not only helped to sell the product but helped to steer the advertising industry in a positive direction. The Hancock campaign redefined slice-of-life advertising and helped to create the decade of the "super," in which we realized we could actually have viewers read our words on television instead of just listen to them. The *1984* Apple commercial simultaneously repositioned Big Blue while it launched Apple and, with its extraordinary execution, also launced an era of mega-productions. Federal Express commercials were a booster rocket for the overnight-package industry. The commercials gave us a disarmingly simple, compelling message guised in a hilarious and scathing look at corporate America. The work was effective enough to turn "Fed-Ex" into a verb; rare indeed. The Rolling Stone campaign gave us a refresher course on minimalism. Perrier gave us a heightened appreciation of geology. With few exceptions, it seems I chose work that not only helped to bolster the clients' image but our own; work that made me a bit prouder to still be in the business.

Joe O'Neill

Advertising's Ten Best Of The Decade 1980-1990

The problem was to create advertising that allowed Federal to break out of the competitive pack as well as the cluttered environment of network television.

We had to focus on the benefits of Federal Express as opposed to detailing the aspects of the service itself, and we had to deliver the message memorably and with humor. We also had to create interest in what was then a historically low interest category.

Strategically it used the backdrop of today's fast paced business world as an avenue to convey Federal's benefit: 'When it absolutely, positively, has to be there overnight.'

Mike Tesch

This commerical came about because I was watching a program called *That's Incredible*. John Moschitta was on the show and he broke the record for talking the fastest of any human. I went into work the next day and said to Mike Tesch, my art director, 'We've got to use this guy for something.'

So we came up with the idea of this executive who talks fast and gets a lot done in one day. We then put every possible cliche of business into his dialogue and the spot turned out to be pretty funny.

Patrick Kelly

"Fast Talker" 1982

ART DIRECTOR
Michael Tesch

WRITER
Patrick Kelly

AGENCY PRODUCER
Maureen Kearns

PRODUCTION COMPANY
Sëdëlmaier Films

DIRECTOR
Joe Sëdëlmaier

CLIENT
Federal Express

AGENCY
Ally & Gargano

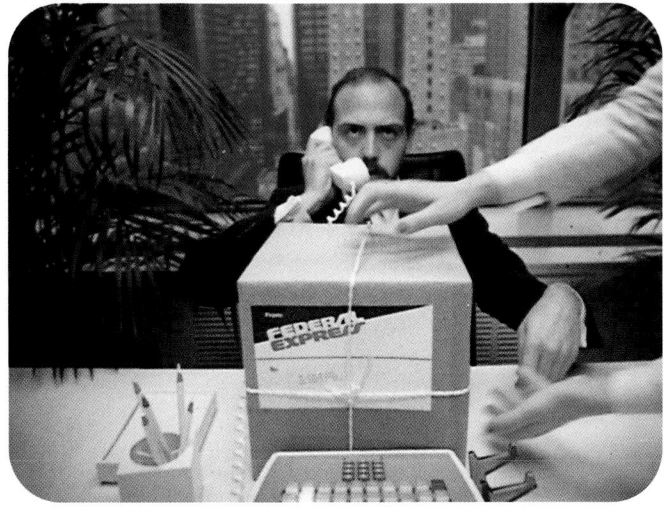

MR SPLEEN VO: Okay Eunice,travelplans.IneedtobeinNewYorkon Monday,LAonTuesday,NewYorkonWednesday,LAonThursday,and NewYorkonFriday.Gotit?Soyouwanttoworkhere,wellwhatmakesyou thinkyoudeserveajobhere?

GUY: Wellsir,Ithinkonmyfeet,I'mgoodwithfiguresandIhaveasharpmind.

SPLEEN: Excellent.CanyoustartMonday?

SPLEEN VO: AndinconclusionJim,Bob,andTed,businessisbusinesssolet's gettowork.Thankyoufortakingthismeeting.PeteryoudidabangupjobI'm puttingyouinchargeofPittsburgh.

PETER: Pittsburgh'sperfect.

SPLEEN: Iknowit'sperfect,Peter,that'swhyIpickedPittsburgh.Pittsburgh's perfect,Peter.MayIcallyouPete?

SPLEEN VO: CongratulationsonyourdealinDenverDavid.I'mputtingyou downtodealinDallas.

ANNCR VO: In this fast moving, high pressure, get-it-done-yesterday world, aren't you glad there's one company that can keep up with it all?
Federal Express.

(SFX)
When it absolutely, positively has to be there overnight.

1984 was the result of having a great product, a brave client, a neat idea and the money to pull it off. In perspective, it was a very special moment in time crystallizing the competition between IBM and Apple.

We were doing something that is very rare in the advertising business — introducing a product that truly was new and revolutionary, and that did not exist until the day Apple put it on sale. Steve Jobs and Apple Computer believed in the product that they had to introduce. They felt it needed a special fanfare and introduction to the world.

We approached the problem with a philosophy that we were introducing a technology which people could use. Fortunately, Apple was as excited about the idea of doing something special as we were.

Brent Thomas, Steve Hayden and I were sitting in my office looking for a blockbuster idea. Brent remembered a Wall Street Journal ad with the headline *Why 1984 won't be like 1984*. We knew there was something there. I drew a board that had one guy sitting in a room watching Big Brother. A girl bursts into the room with a baseball bat and smashes the TV. Then Brent got much more elaborate with his Orwellian vision . . .

Lee Clow

In retrospect, what strikes me is how quickly it all happened. We were struggling with the notion of an introductory spot for Macintosh, and I happened upon an old print idea that had been written (in vain, as it turned out) the year before for the Wall Street Journal campaign: *Why 1984 won't be like 1984*.

They (Steve Jobs) hated it, I was told. Too cerebral, or something. 'But it's a great idea,' I replied, 'and it's built for film. Think of the theater lurking within the concept'

Steve did, and so did Lee Clow.

We worked on it for half an hour or so, and I was dispatched from Lee's office with a script that Hank Hinton, the storyboard artist, translated into a piece of film.

Total time was about four hours.

Brent Thomas

'Why 1984 almost wasn't like anything.' A True Story by Steve Hayden

Why 1984 won't be like 1984 was a line from a never-produced ad done by Gary Gussick and Mike Moser which Brent Thomas and I purloined for our purposes. It was the inspiration for the whole spot. Our own suits tried to keep us from shooting a 60 version, because the client had only signed an estimate for a 30. Without authorization, I authorized it.

After the spot was finished, Apple's board was appalled. The only reason *1984* aired was because we were unable to sell off $500,000 worth of Super Bowl time and had to fill 60 seconds with something. So we really owe it all to the ineptness of Chiat/Day's media department.

Steve Hayden

"1984" 1984
ART DIRECTORS
Brent Thomas
Lee Clow
WRITER
Steve Hayden
AGENCY PRODUCER
Richard O'Neill
PRODUCTION COMPANY
Fairbanks Films
DIRECTOR
Ridley Scott
CLIENT
Apple Computer
AGENCY
Chiat/Day - Los Angeles

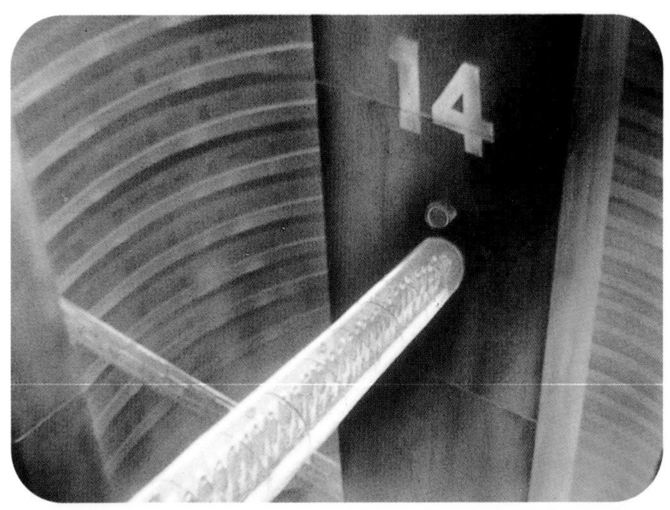

VO: Today we celebrate the first glorious anniversary of the Information Purification Directives.
We have created, for the first time in all history, a garden of pure ideology, where each worker may bloom secure from the pests of contradictory and confusing truths.
Our Unification of Thought is more powerful a weapon than any fleet or army on earth.
We are one people. With one will. One resolve. One cause.
Our enemies shall talk themselves to death. And we will bury them with their own confusion.
We shall prevail.

ANNCR VO: On January 24, 1984, Apple Computer will introduce Macintosh and you'll see why 1984 won't be like 1984.

The original *Rolling Stone* campaign was one of those rare instances where the solution to the client's problem was absolutely obvious.

The creative team had the foresight to tell it straight. The account team had the intelligence to leave it alone. And the client had the faith and the guts to run it.

Nancy Rice

The *Perception/Reality* campaign changed the way I think about what I do.

I am a writer. But words aren't enough to describe what I do.

For me, this campaign stands as the clearest example of what the real difference is between an art director and a writer.

Where there is a good idea, the boundaries between art director and writer collapse. The definitions blur.

I don't sell headlines. I sell ideas.

I am an idea man.

If I had a nickel for every headline that I wrote for this campaign, I'd be worth a dime.

Bill Miller

"Perception Reality Campaign" 1986
ART DIRECTOR
Nancy Rice
WRITER
Bill Miller
PHOTOGRAPHERS
Mark Hauser
Jim Marvy
CLIENT
Rolling Stone
AGENCY
Fallon McElligott/
Minneapolis

Perception.

Reality.

If your idea of a Rolling Stone reader looks like a holdout from the 60's, welcome to the 80's.
Rolling Stone ranks number one in reaching concentrations of 18-34 readers with household incomes exceeding $25,000. When you buy Rolling Stone, you buy an audience that sets the trends and shapes the buying patterns for the most affluent consumers in America. That's the kind of reality you can take to the bank.

Perception.

Reality.

If you still think a Rolling Stone reader's idea of standard equipment is flowers on the door panels and incense in the ashtrays, consider this: Rolling Stone households own 5,199,000 automobiles.
If you've got cars to sell, welcome to the fast lane.

Rolling Stone

Perception.

Reality.

If you think the pages of Rolling Stone are filled with left wing politics and music to make your hair stand on end, call 1-212-PL8-3800 and we'll send you a copy of America's #1 lifestyle publication for 18-34 year olds, featuring the latest and most respected information about what's happening in music and entertainment today.
If you're not on the cover of Rolling Stone, don't worry, there's still room inside. Source: Simmons 1984

We spent a lot of time walking around with telephone books (usually in restaurants or bars where they thought we were going to sell them space). It started as a fun kind of mind game that just snowballed. Though I like the spots that won, my favorite non-produced spot was titled *Interior Decorators.* A house painter labors over mixing just the right color. Then he drinks it. Unfortunately, the networks said 'Nahhhh.'

Marty Weiss

The campaign was based on a simple observation: Anything you can imagine can be found between the covers of a NYNEX Yellow Pages. And many things you can't. After bringing the concept to radio and outdoor, the question became how to make it live on TV?

What else? We did the natural thing and resorted to bad puns. Then we staged them simply so nothing would get in the way of their innate dumbness. It became a game for viewers, and for all of us involved in the campaign's creation. And in the end, that's where I believe the strength of the campaign resided. Between a great agency and a great client who, above all else, like to have fun together.

Robin Raj

"Dumbwaiters, Rock Drills, Furniture Stripping" 1988

ART DIRECTOR
Marty Weiss

WRITER
Robin Raj

AGENCY PRODUCERS
Mark Sitley
Steve Amato

PRODUCTION COMPANIES
Directing Artists
Fernbach Productions

DIRECTORS
Kevin Godley
Lol Creme
Alex Fernbach

CLIENT
NYNEX

AGENCY
Chiat/Day

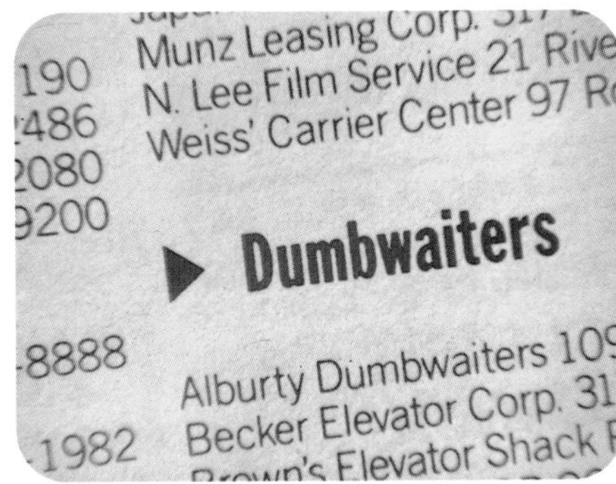

(SFX: OPENING CHIME; RESTAURANT SOUNDS)

MVO: Excuse me . . .

WAITER: Sir!

MVO: What are your specials today?

WAITER: I don't know.

FVO: Do your entrees come with salad?

WAITER: I don't know.

FVO: Do you have escargots?

WAITER: Escargots? (PAUSE) I don't know.

FVO: May we see a menu?

WAITER (CONFUSED): Yes! No! I don't know.

VO: If it's out there, it's in here . . .
(SFX: PLATES BREAKING)
The NYNEX Yellow Pages.
(SFX: BOOK SLAMS SHUT)
Why would anyone need another?

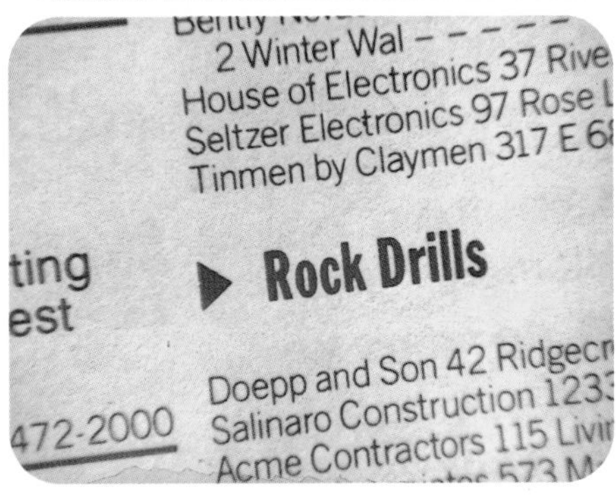

(SFX: OPENING CHIME; SOUND OF MARCHING)

OFF-CAMERA SERGEANT (YELLING): Atten Hut! Funky Chicken.

(SFX: MILITARY SNARE DRUM THROUGHOUT)

SARGE: Duckwalk! . . . Moonwalk! . . . Disco! . . . Windmill! . . . Air Guitar! . . . James Brown!

SOLDIERS (YELLING TOGETHER): Huh!

SARGE: Jimi plays Monterey!

VO: If it's out there, it's in here . . . The NYNEX Yellow Pages.
(SFX: BOOK SLAMS SHUT)
Why would anyone need another?

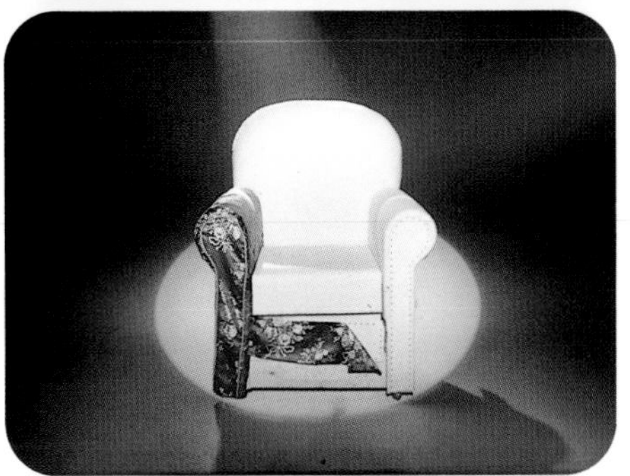

(SFX: OPENING CHIME; AS LIGHTS GO DOWN, STRIPPER MUSIC BEGINS; CLAPPING; WHISTLING)

(SFX: MUSIC AND CROWD NOISE CONTINUE)

(SFX: MUSIC AND CROWD NOISE CONTINUE; SOUND OF SPRINGS POPPING OFF)

(SFX: MUSIC AND CROWD NOISE CONTINUE)

VO: If it's out there, it's in here . . .
(SFX: CAT CALL WHISTLE)
The NYNEX Yellow Pages.
(SFX: BOOK SLAMS SHUT)
Why would anyone need another?

Like most campaigns that attract an unusual amount of attention, the Bartles and Jaymes advertising broke a lot of "rules." We dreamed up an improbable name, chose as spokesmen two guys who were about as unlike the target audience as you could get, and asked our client for his agreement to produce, on the average, a new commercial each week.

Fortunately, we had one of those rare clients who endorses risk, and who shared our hope of hitting a home run. Research didn't offer us a lot of reassurance, as about half the respondents thought it was one of the dumbest ideas they'd ever seen, while the rest were puzzled. Nevertheless, we produced some inexpensive spots, put them in test market, and got nearly a 50 percent share of the market in less that a month.

Why did it work? Partly, I think, because a good part of the audience saw it as a humorous spoof on marketing and advertising, which we hoped it was. Partly because an entirely different group of people simply saw Frank and Ed as two natural and disarming characters. And partly because it was just different enough to stand out from all the other stuff on the air.

When we were just getting started with production, I asked David Rufkahr, the Oregon farmer we had cast as Frank Bartles, what he might wish for in his wildest dreams. He said, 'A drill press.' I think he got one.

Hal Riney

Actually, the most exciting thing for me about the Bartles and Jaymes campaign was the opportunity to do so many spots. (I think about 150 altogether.)

It meant that if you had one that didn't turn out so well, you knew that next month you could quickly make up for it.

Looking back, I think there were three or four commercials that never ran. They were probably some of the best work. Darn. I wish people could have seen those.

Jerry Andelin

"Introduction Campaign" 1986

ART DIRECTOR
Gerald Andelin

WRITER
Hal Riney

AGENCY PRODUCER
Deborah Martin

PRODUCTION COMPANY
Pytka

DIRECTOR
Joe Pytka

CLIENT
E&J Gallo Winery

AGENCY
Hal Riney & Partners/
San Francisco

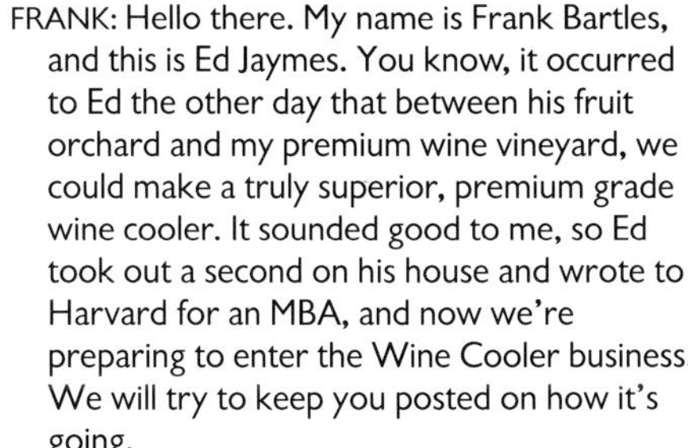

FRANK: Hello there. My name is Frank Bartles, and this is Ed Jaymes. You know, it occurred to Ed the other day that between his fruit orchard and my premium wine vineyard, we could make a truly superior, premium grade wine cooler. It sounded good to me, so Ed took out a second on his house and wrote to Harvard for an MBA, and now we're preparing to enter the Wine Cooler business. We will try to keep you posted on how it's going.
Thank you very much for your support.

FRANK: Hello again. I'm Frank Bartles, and you remember Ed Jaymes, my partner. We have selected a bottle for our new premium wine cooler, and we were about to print up a label when Ed called my attention to the fact that we did not yet have a name for our product. We were lucky he noticed that, as that would have been a big mistake.
So if you have any good ideas for a wine cooler name, we'd really appreciate your sending them along.
Thank you again for your support.

FRANK: We want to thank you for all the name suggestions for our new wine cooler. There were some really clever ones. But we decided just to call it "The Bartles and Jaymes Wine Cooler" because my name is Bartles, and Ed's is Jaymes.If you don't like the name, please don't tell us because we have already printed up our labels.
Anyway, you could always just call it Bartles and skip the Jaymes all together.
Ed says that is okay with him.
Thanks for your continued support.

The *501 Blues* was a campaign that could have gone on forever, evolving and changing every year as the attitudes, interests, and styles of young people changed.

It was like the Eleven O'Clock News—you didn't think about the format because the *content* always changed.

Unfortunately, the campaign's success probably led to its demise. It was imitated out of existence.

Leslie Caldwell

What a run. Five years, 90 different commercials, each with its own original piece of music. For me, every spot was the ultimate collaboration between writer, art director, producer and director. Any one of us could veto any piece of music, any lyric, any scene, any prospective cast member—for any reason. And for five years, there was not a single storyboard frame drawn. Levi's trusted us to produce good commercials that were always in their best interest.

In my entire career, I've never worked so hard. Or had so much fun.

Mike Koelker

"Gang, Blues Singer, Street Singers" 1985
ART DIRECTORS
Chris Blum
Leslie Caldwell
WRITER
Mike Koelker
AGENCY PRODUCER
Steve Neely
PRODUCTION COMPANY
Petermann/Dektor
DIRECTOR
Leslie Dektor
CLIENT
Levi Strauss
AGENCY
Foote Cone & Belding/
San Francisco

SINGER VO: *Shrink to fit only you.*

SINGERS VO: *501 Blues.*

SINGER: *Do the things that you do.*

GROUP: *501 Blues.*

SINGER: *Fit a personal way.*

GROUP: *501 Blues*

SINGER: *Wear 'em every day.*

GROUP: *501 Blues.*

SINGER: *Nothin' like these jeans,*
The coolest jeans I've seen,
501 Blues.
Levi's button-fly
501 Blues.

SINGER: *Ain't no body*
Like my body
That's about the size of it.
So I personalize my size
With Levi's 501 Blues
They shrink to fit.
They're the blues that make me feel good,
Levi's 501 Blues.
Love them Blues!
Oh yeah!

SINGERS VO: *Shrink to fit*
And a button fly, too
Aah-Ooh
Levi's 501 Blues.
Shrink your own
Very personal pair
A little loose here
And a little tight there.
We're so blue
We've got the blues
So blue
The 501 Blues.
We're so blue
Levi's 501 Blues.

LEAD SINGER: *Hahaha.*

Like most Federal spots, this one made its point by poking fun at its customers. But what was really funny was that the more we did it, the more the customers liked it.

Mike Tesch

This commercial came about in an effort to show people how easy it is to use Federal Express.

Federal was new at this time and a lot of people thought it was complicated, or that they had to go through a freight forwarder, or something like that.

So we did this spot to explain how easy the whole thing was. It was also a way to put down executives and the tendency toward the 'higher up in the company you go, the less you have to do or know.' We were appealing to low-level executives and we thought they would get a kick out of this.

Patrick Kelly

"Easy To Use" 1980

ART DIRECTOR
Michael Tesch
WRITER
Patrick Kelly
AGENCY PRODUCER
Maureen Kearns
PRODUCTION COMPANY
Sëdëlmaier Films
DIRECTOR
Joe Sëdëlmaier
CLIENT
Federal Express
AGENCY
Ally & Gargano

ANNCR VO: A lot of people think using Federal Express is complicated but really, it's so simple, even a vice-president can do it.

VP VO: Helloooo Federal.

ANNCR VO: All you do is pick up the phone and we come to your office and pick up the package. Why, even a president can do that!

PRESIDENT VO: Helloooo Federal.

ANNCR VO: In fact, using Federal Express is so simple that even a chairman of the board can do it.

CHAIRMAN VO: Helloooo . . .

(SFX: FINGERS, SNAP, SNAP)

ANNCR VO: Federal Express. When it absolutely, positively has to be there overnight.

In early 1984, Nike sent Chiat/Day a memo stating that they wanted to deal directly with the creative people, not 'pin-striped, zoot-suited account executives.' This was a rare client. One who wouldn't need to be cajoled and pleaded with to buy unusual work. Gary Johns art directed most of the billboards, I did a few of them. But it was Lee Clow, who with a pair of scissors and a pile of *Sports Illustrated* magazines would give birth to the idea.

The day of the Nike presentation came around and a massive sign was put up in our lobby. It read: 'ABSOLUTELY NO PIN-STRIPED, ZOOT-SUITED ACCOUNT EXECUTIVES ALLOWED BEYOND THIS POINT.'

Houman Pirdavari

When Nike asked Chiat/Day to design a campaign for the L.A. Olympics, we felt that billboards had to be a part of it. This was, after all, L.A., and we figured people would spend more time in their cars going to the events than at them.

The idea was to make Nike seem like they were the sponsor of the Olympics, even though they weren't the "official" sponsor.

We also wanted to make a very non-commerical statement. Therefore, there were no sweeping statements and no tag-lines. We reasoned that the visual statements of athletes sweating and doing their thing would say more about Nike's work-ethic philosophy than all the headlines in the world. You know, one picture is worth a thousand words. Also, it was an international event. Not everybody would be speaking the same language.

One day, we were on the UCLA campus and happened to be talking to a complete stranger, someone who didn't know we were in advertising, let alone the creators of the campaign. He was remarking that on the way over, on the 405 Freeway, he had just seen this fantastic billboard. He couldn't figure out what it was about or who had sponsored it, and to his own amazement, he got off at the next exit, got back on the freeway, and straining to see the logo, noticed it was Nike.

It was our first indication that we had come up with something that might just work.

Jeff Gorman
Gary Johns

What should a writer say about outdoor boards with no headlines?

Brent Bouchez

Nike Outdoor Campaign 1984
ART DIRECTORS
Gary Johns
Houman Pirdavari
WRITER
Brent Bouchez
PHOTOGRAPHER
Focus On Sports
CLIENT
Nike
AGENCY
Chiat/Day - Los Angeles

NIKE

NIKE

NIKE

Both the outdoor and *I Love L.A.* were a celebration of the athlete and the '84 Olympics, brought to you by a company dedicated to people doing things athletic. The "non-advertising" attitude spoke to an intelligent audience in a "cool" way.

People could speak for ten minutes about what a "cool" company Nike was—what cool products they made—and we didn't even show a shoe. Nike has continued to do cool advertising and make cool products; I think any guy on the street would tell you that 'Nike is cool.'

The interesting thing is when the guys from Nike came to us the first time, they said, 'Nike is a cool company. We make neat stuff and we want to do some cool ads.' Neat strategy, huh?

Lee Clow

If you ever wanted proof that there's a cosmic mind, this television commercial could be entered as Exhibit A.

Right after Chiat/Day had been invited to create a campaign for Nike during the 1984 Olympics, we were heading down the Santa Monica Freeway, when we had an idea: How about using the newly released video, *I Love L.A.* and stick in Nike's athletes and the billboards we were creating, to make a 60-second TV spot that would be more music video than commercial.

When we got back to the office, we found out that Lee Clow had had the same idea. So had Gene Cameron, an account guy. Later, we learned that both other agencies who pitched the account, Hal Riney and Wieden and Kennedy, had come up with the same thought. Not only that, but the client, Nike, had thought of it, too.

We looked at each other and thought if all these other people had the same idea, how good could it be?

After a lot of agonizing and soul searching, the commercial got made . . . and went on to win every major award, including this latest honor.

Which proves that if a client or account executive has the same idea as you, don't disregard it out of hand.

It might be cosmic.

Jeff Gorman
Gary Johns

"I Love LA" 1984

ART DIRECTORS
Lee Clow
Gary Johns

WRITER
Jeff Gorman

AGENCY PRODUCER
Morty Baran

PRODUCTION COMPANIES
Jenkins Covington Newman
Directors Consortium

DIRECTORS
Tim Newman
Mark Coppos

CLIENT
Nike

AGENCY
Chiat/Day - Los Angeles

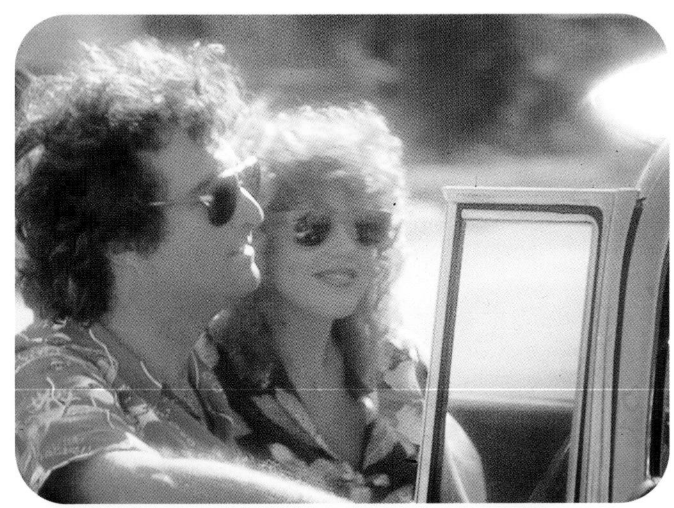

(MUSIC THROUGHOUT: "I LOVE LA")

RANDY NEWMAN: *Rollin' down Imperial Highway. A big nasty red-head at my side. Santa Ana winds blowin' hot from the north. We was born to ride. From the South Bay, to the Valley. From the West Side, to the East Side. Everybody's very happy 'cause the sun is shining all the time. It's like another perfect day. I love LA!*

CHORUS: *We love it!*

RANDY NEWMAN: *We love it!*

CHORUS: *Ah, ah, ah, ah . . .*

RANDY NEWMAN: *I love LA!*

CHORUS: *We love it!*

The client wanted a heritage campaign.

We politely reminded him he'd only been in business two years: he had no heritage.

As it turned out, that wasn't true. People had been concocting this stuff in tubs on the beaches of California long before it was ever bottled.

So we talked to those people, watched old surf movies, listened to rock n' roll and drank a cooler or two.

Then we wrote about what we had learned.

Now some people are saying these ads have an important place in advertising history in the '80s.

We look at it as the best vacation we've ever had.

Dave Woodside
Dave O'Hare
Mike Moser

I used to mix this stuff up on the beach when I surfed for a living, and these guys put it in a bottle. I figured that showing people the rich heritage of the product (à la "Beechwood aging," or "selling no wine before its time") would capture the quality experience in every bottle.

I was technical consultant as well as creative director on this one.

Lee Clow

"Meet the People, The Chairman, Up and Down the Coast" 1987

ART DIRECTORS
Mike Moser
David Bigman
Lee Clow

WRITERS
Dave O'Hare
Dave Woodside

AGENCY PRODUCER
Francesca Cohn

PRODUCTION COMPANY
Coppos Films

DIRECTOR
Mark Coppos

CLIENT
California Cooler

AGENCY
Chiat/Day -
San Francisco

ANNCR VO: Meet the people who made the original wine coolers.

(MUSIC UP: "SURFIN' BIRD" THROUGHOUT)

California white wine and real fruit
Blended in a tub.
At a party.
On the beach.
And now that original blend comes in a bottle.

(MUSIC: GURGLING PART OF SONG)

California Cooler. The real stuff.

(MUSIC: "GIMME SOME LOVIN" THROUGHOUT)

ANNCR VO: For years, it was made by guys with names like Rabbit, Quasimodo, The Chairman.
Real fruit.
And California white wine.

SINGERS: *Hey!*

ANNCR VO: Real fruit and white wine.
Blended under ideal conditions.

(MUSIC: LYRICS UP)

California Cooler.
The Real Stuff.
Now in bottles.

(MUSIC UP: "GREEN ONIONS" THROUGHOUT)

ANNCR VO: Up and down the coast of California, the locals made a drink they called cooler. Using white wine and real fruit, they made it on beaches like Rincon, Swami's, San Onofre, The Ranch.
And now that original blend comes in a bottle, and you'll find it in places like Shreveport, Newark, Des Moines, Boise . . .
(FADE)

Our strategy on Miller Lite was to sell it not as a "diet beer" but as a real beer drinker's beer. So Dick Butkus and Bubba Smith, two of the most ferocious football players of all time, were ideal spokesmen for our cause. They could dress up in tuxedos and talk about going to the opera, but it was easy to see that they felt more at home in a good bar with a good beer in their hands.

Whereas most Miller Lite spokesmen were some of the best players of their time, Bob Uecker may have been the worst. But we portrayed Bob as a man who desperately wanted the same adulation that great athletes receive. After all, he drank the same beer as them.

In the first spot he did for us, Bob was locked out of the bar. He solved that in this commercial by pretending to be Whitey Ford. The next commercial we did with Bob was the one we thought was the best—*I Must Be in the Front Row.*

By the way, the commercials Dick, Bubba and Bob did for Miller Lite helped them get their own TV series and numerous parts in feature films. And helped Miller Lite become the seond-largest selling beer in America. I guess advertising really does work.

Charlie Breen
Nick Gisonde

Umpire Jim Honochick's poor eyesight gave Ed Butler and me a great opportunity to do a commercial with a visual gag. A ketchup bottle, being similar to a beer bottle, was the perfect prop.

Ed and I choreographed the commercial over lunch one day.

On shoot day, Steve Horn had Honochick and Powell so well rehearsed that the shoot ended by mid-afternoon. Three bottles of Clark's ketchup were produced for the shoot. I still have two.

Dave Clark

It was April 1983, not Christmas.

Yet Charlie Breen and Nick Gisonde gave me this wonderful gift. They asked me to take a crack at a Miller Lite script.

I had this goofy idea. What would happen if squinty old umpire Jim Honochick mistook a bottle of ketchup for a bottle of Miller Lite?

Dave Clark and I put the idea on a storyboard. Steve Horn put it on film. And Boog Powell played the perfect straightman.

Working on Miller Lite began as a happy accident (I had been writing ads for Campbell's Soup), and ended up a labor of love.

Which is saying a lot coming from a guy who hasn't had a drink in eight years.

Ed Butler

"Butkus, Uecker, Powell" 1984

ART DIRECTORS
Nick Gisonde
Dave Clark

WRITERS
Charlie Breen
Ed Butler

AGENCY PRODUCERS
Tom Dakin
Eric Steinhauser
Marc Mayhew

PRODUCTION COMPANIES
Steve Horn Productions
Bob Giraldi Productions

DIRECTORS
Steve Horn
Bob Giraldi

CLIENT
Miller Brewing/Lite Beer

AGENCY
Backer & Spielvogel

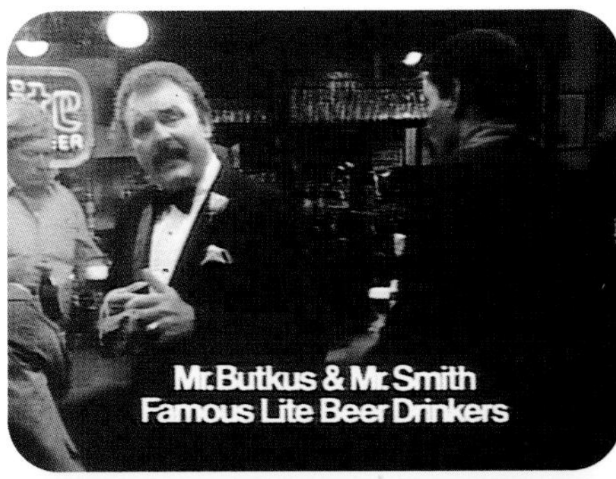

(SFX: BAR SOUNDS)

BUTKUS: I tell ya, trying to get cultured isn't easy. We just went to the opera, and we didn't understand a word.

SMITH: Yeah. That big guy in those tights sure could sing.

BUTKUS: Well, at least we still drink a very civilized beer. Lite Beer from Miller. Lite tastes great.

SMITH: But us impresarios drink it because it's less filling.

BUTKUS: We can't afford to get filled up. Tomorrow night we're going to the ballet.

SMITH: Yeah, I sure hope they do it in English.

(SFX: CROWD LAUGHS)

ANNCR VO: Lite Beer from Miller. Everything you always wanted in a beer. And less.

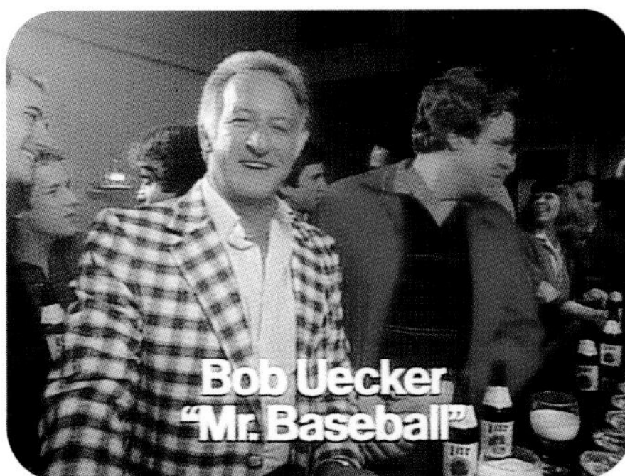

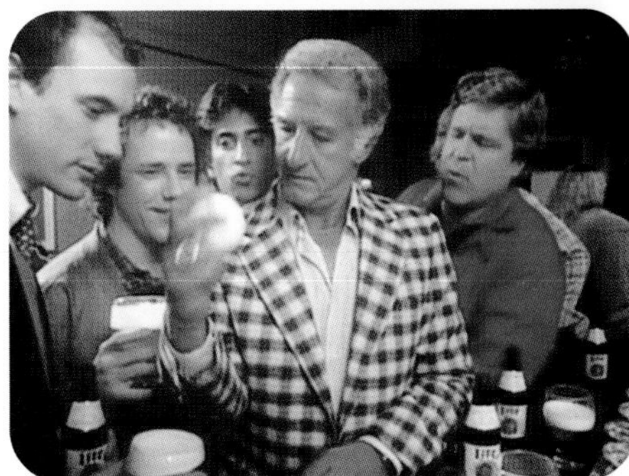

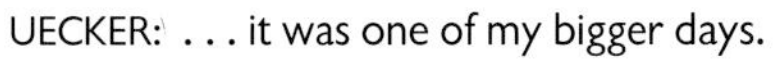

UECKER: . . . it was one of my bigger days.

MAN: Let me buy you a beer.

UECKER: Sure.
Ah, these fans, I love 'em. When I came in, they didn't recognize me at first. But then when I told them who I was, next thing you know they're buying me my favorite beer. Lite Beer from Miller. They know us ex-big-leaguers drink Lite because it's got a third less calories than their regular beer. It's less filling, and it tastes great.
Thanks.

MAN: Hey, it's a pleasure to buy a beer for a great pitcher like Whitey Ford.

UECKER: So I lied.

ANNCR VO: Lite Beer from Miller. Everything you always wanted in a beer. And less.

MAN: Hey, Whitey, I thought you were a lefty.

UECKER: Ooo, that's right.

BOOG: For years now we've been kidding Jim about his eyesight. The fact is, Jim has the eyes of an eagle.

JIM: Thanks Boog.

BOOG: Why, he was one of the first guys to spot Lite Beer from Miller. Saw right away that Lite tastes great and is less filling.

JIM: Sure, all you have to do is read the label. It says that Lite has one third less calories than their regular beer.

BOOG: I think you want this, Jim.

JIM: Oh, yeah. Thanks Boog. As I was saying, it's as plain as the nose on your face . . .

ANNCR VO: Lite Beer from Miller. Everything you always wanted in a beer. And less.

BOOG: Oh, I don't believe this.

When I first wrote the script for what has become *Where's the Beef?* it was originally entitled *Fluffy Bun.* And no wonder. When I originally presented the script *all* the laughs were on the lines 'It certainly is a big bun . . . big fluffy bun . . .' Nobody, but nobody was laughing on 'Where's the beef?' Of course, that was before Joe Sëdëlmaier introduced us to Clara Peller and her voice and her personality.

Does anyone know there was another *Where's the Beef?* shot at the same time? With an all-male cast? It's pretty good too — only nobody ever saw it. I wonder how the actors must feel.

Cliff Freeman

"Where's the Beef?" 1984

ART DIRECTOR
Donna Weinheim

WRITER
Cliff Freeman

AGENCY PRODUCER
Susan Scherl

PRODUCTION COMPANY
Sëdëlmaier Films

DIRECTOR
Joe Sëdëlmaier

CLIENT
Wendy's

AGENCY
Dancer-Fitzgerald-Sample

MILDRED: It certainly is a *big* bun.

ELIZABETH: It's a *very* big bun.

MILDRED: A big *fluffy* bun.

ELIZABETH (WEAKER): A . . . very . . . big . . . fluffy . . . bun.

CLARA: Where's the beef?

ANNCR VO: Some hamburger places give you a lot less beef on a lot of bun.

CLARA: Where's the beef?

ANNCR VO: At Wendy's, we serve a hamburger we modestly call a "Single" – and Wendy's Single has more beef than the Whopper or Big Mac. At Wendy's, you get more beef and less bun.

CLARA: Hey, where's the beef? I don't think there's anybody back there!

ANNCR VO: You want something better, you're Wendy's kind of people.

Advertising's Ten Best Of The Decade 1980-1990

Finalists: Print, Radio, Television

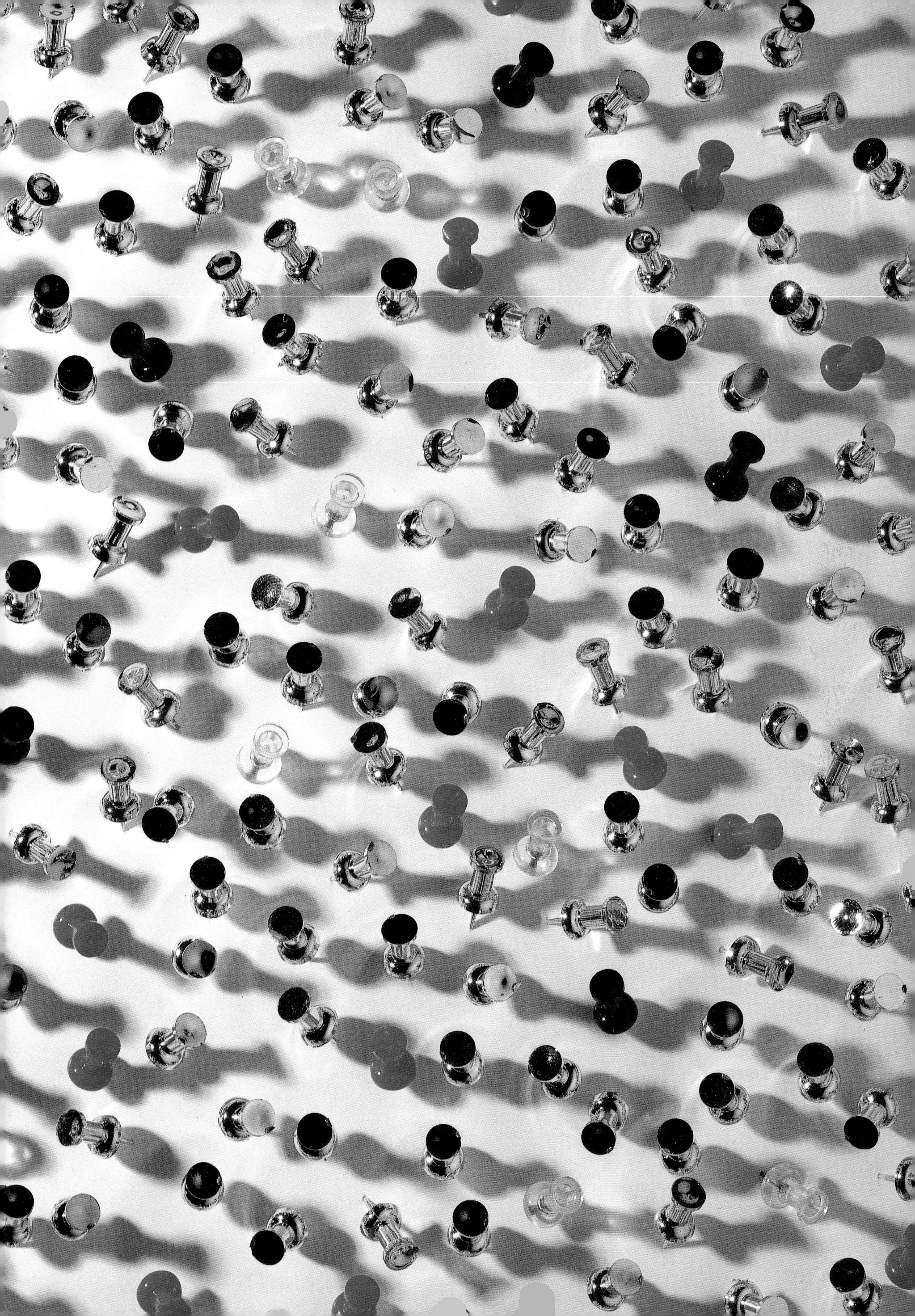

AFTER 500 PLAYS OUR HIGH FIDELITY TAPE STILL DELIVERS HIGH FIDELITY.

If your old favorites don't sound as good as they used to, the problem could be your recording tape.

Some tapes show their age more than others. And when a tape ages prematurely, the music on it does too.

What can happen is, the oxide particles that are bound onto tape loosen and fall off, taking some of your music with them.

At Maxell, we've developed a binding process that helps to prevent this. When oxide particles are bound onto our tape, they stay put. And so does your music.

So even after a Maxell recording is 500 plays old, you'll swear it's not a play over five.

IT'S WORTH IT.

IF THERE'S A MAXELL CASSETTE IN THIS CAR AND IT DOESN'T WORK, WE'LL REPLACE IT.

If you own a car stereo, you've probably already discovered that many cassette tapes don't last as long in your car as they do in your living room.

Conditions like heat, cold, humidity, and even potholes can contribute to a cassette's premature demise.

At Maxell, our cassette shells are built to standards that are as much as 60% higher than the industry calls for. Which is why we can offer you the best guarantee in the industry. An unconditional lifetime warranty.

So if you'd like better mileage out of your cassette tape, try Maxell. Even after 100,000 miles on the road, it'll run like new.

If only they made cars this well.

IT'S WORTH IT.

WHAT'S
HAPPENING
ON THIS PAGE
SHOULDN'T
HAPPEN
ON YOUR
RECORDING
TAPE.

It's called print-through.
And if you think it interferes with your reading, you should hear what it does to your listening.

It happens on tape that has low magnetic stability. Music on one layer of the tape is transferred to music on an adjacent layer, causing an echo.

At Maxell, we've designed our tape for superior magnetic stability. So what's happening to the opposite page won't happen to your music.

You see, we believe you should only hear the music you want to hear. Nothing less, and nothing more.

IT'S WORTH IT.

1981

ART DIRECTOR
Lars Anderson

WRITER
Peter Levathes

DESIGNER
Lars Anderson

PHOTOGRAPHER
Steve Steigman

CLIENT
Maxell

AGENCY
Scali McCabe Sloves

INTRODUCING THE FORERUNNER OF IMITATIONS TO COME.

THE NEW BMW 528e.

It seems the automotive establishment has caught up with automotive enthusiasts in their affection for BMW's.

Lately, affection has become ardor—as witnessed by the number of cars resembling BMW's, comparing themselves to BMW's, and even claiming to perform "like" BMW's.

BMW shares this vision of what a car should be in the eighties, with one major disclaimer: cars should be motivated by foresight, not hindsight. And no better example exists than the new, technologically advanced BMW 528e.

THE 1982 CAR THAT WON'T BE IRRELEVANT BY 1987.

The new 528e is a luxury performance sedan that escapes further categorization largely because its category doesn't exist yet.

It is the sort of car other car makers, or those of them who value performance, will someday have to attempt—one that turns minimum energy into maximum performance.

The 528e accomplishes this through an inspired paradox called the "Eta" engine.

It runs slower than conventional 6-cylinder engines, stretching fuel in the process. Yet at the same time, it develops higher torque (or power) at those slower engine speeds—speeds at which the car is most often driven.

The result is the sort of exhilarating engine response you would expect if fuel efficiency were no obstacle; because in the 528e, it isn't.

Deep within the engine, where the important fuel efficiency decisions are made, another BMW innovation makes sure those decisions are always made in favor of maximum performance.

Digital Motor Electronics is an electronic system that constantly monitors the engine and assures that fuel ignition occurs at the optimum moment. It also cuts off fuel flow to cylinders when they're not needed, allowing the car to run on its own momentum during deceleration, saving fuel for acceleration.

All this makes for a car that performs extraordinarily well because of the fact that it's extraordinarily efficient, not in spite of it. Which helps explain its mileage figures, unsurpassed by any gasoline-powered car in its price class: EPA-estimated [22] mpg, 32 mpg highway.*

ONE OF THE WORLD'S MOST OBEDIENT AUTOMOBILES.

The eighties are already being touted as the era of the personal car, a time when driver regains mastery over automobile.

As trailblazers forge ahead in this direction, they'll find the trail has been previously blazed by the 528e.

Its suspension is a refinement of a design so advanced, Car and Driver termed it "the single most significant breakthrough in front suspension design in this decade."

The resulting agility is complemented by its steering, highly responsive in the manner of all BMW's (a legacy of its racing forebears). On the road, it is one of the most obedient cars in the world.

Inside, it is a model of the "new" science of ergonomics, a recent discovery with some car makers and a tradition at BMW.

The interior is an elegant continuum of driver and automobile created by easily accessible controls, contoured seats and many other functional amenities.

But despite all this, no claim is made for the 528e as the Car of the Future.

It is not a car designed for mass-market accolades, but rather for a finite number of serious drivers—enthusiasts who've watched the performance characteristics of cars diminish in tandem with the world's fuel supply.

For those people, the 528e may well be a deliverance.

You may judge for yourself at your BMW dealer, where the 528e awaits your test drive.

THE ULTIMATE DRIVING MACHINE.
BMW MUNICH, GERMANY

*Figures are for comparison purposes only. Actual mileage may vary, depending on speed, weather and trip length; actual highway mileage will most likely be lower. © 1982 BMW of North America, Inc. The BMW trademark and logo are registered trademarks of Bayerische Motoren Werke, A.G.

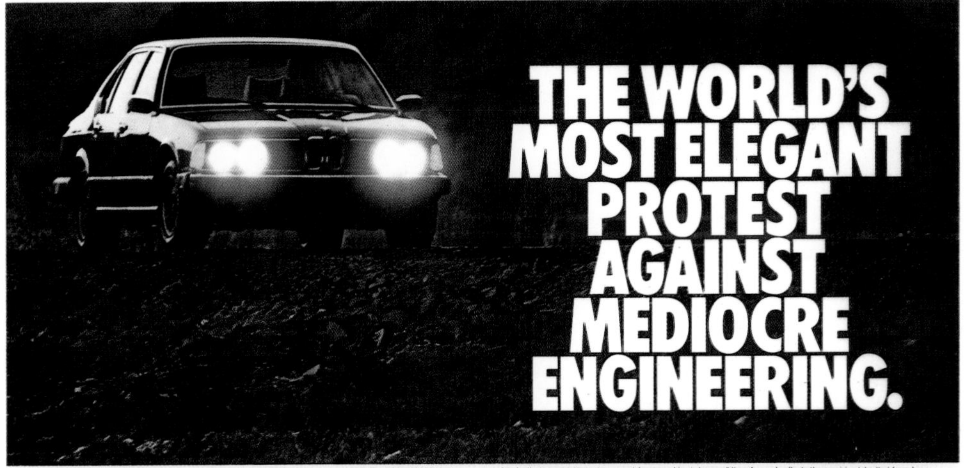

The protest we have in mind is against prestigious luxury cars that succeed as symbols, but disappoint as cars.

Cars whose underlying engineering seems to have lagged behind their considerable reputations.

Luxury car buyers dissatisfied with this state of affairs will find a perfect vehicle for dissent in the BMW 733i—the $35,000 luxury car engineered to lead where others have lagged.

INTRODUCING DIGITAL MOTOR ELECTRONICS.

The 733i is the first automobile in America to offer Digital Motor Electronics—a system that illustrates the difference between technology and gadgetry.

"DME" measures, reports on and, most importantly, governs engine efficiency.

It assures that the optimum mixture of fuel and air is ignited at the optimum time in the ignition cycle. It adjusts idling speed, cuts off fuel flow to cylinders when they're not needed, and even helps report back, through a fuel economy indicator, your actual mpg figures as you drive.

The figures will make interesting reading. The 733i with standard five-speed transmission now delivers a pleasantly surprising [19] EPA estimated mpg, 29 mpg highway. Automatic is also available.

(Fuel efficiency figures are for comparison purposes only. Your actual mileage may vary, depending on speed, weather and trip length. Your actual highway mileage will most likely be lower.)

Inside, an onboard computer provides such useful functions as anti-theft protection and speed monitoring—and even helps control the weather. A special climate control adjusts temperatures to a preset level, going so far as to warn you of potential icing conditions.

All these technological advances accompany a car that's fairly steeped in amenities.

Its molded bucket seats are upholstered in wide rolls of fine leather. Carpeting is thick and plush. And the attentiveness to comfort throughout caused Car and Driver to single out the 733i as "the height of refined elegance."

PERFECTION IS UNATTAINABLE. SUPERIORITY ISN'T.

Of course, the true measure of any machine is how well it performs—an axiom that confers an almost unfair advantage on the 733i.

Its 3.2-liter, electronically fuel-injected engine has been called "without a doubt, the most sophisticated production in-line six in the world" (Road & Track magazine), delivering the exhilarating performance that's conspicuously absent among cars in its class.

Its revolutionary double-pivot front suspension is so advanced it has been awarded an international patent.

And its amazingly agile steering reflects the precision inherited from over six decades of building high-performance vehicles.

The sum, according to Car and Driver, is a car whose "parts and pieces...work so well together they must have been melded in another world."

If your present luxury sedan suggests more mundane origins, you might contact your nearest BMW dealer, who will be happy to arrange a test drive at your convenience.

THE ULTIMATE DRIVING MACHINE.
BMW, MUNICH, GERMANY

© 1981 BMW of North America, Inc. The BMW trademark and logo are registered trademarks of Bayerische Motoren Werke, A.G.

BMW. ONE OF THE FEW CAR COMPANIES NOT CURRENTLY INTRODUCING IMITATION BMW'S.

The annual new-car introductions have ushered in cars so strongly resembling BMW's as to suggest new meaning for the term 'coincidence.'

And a good many of these newcomers claim (small surprise) to perform 'like' a BMW.

This sudden enthusiasm for BMW-like performance is flattering—and amusing.

Because while it's possible to develop enthusiasm virtually overnight, the development of engineering takes considerably longer—a fact that's amply demonstrated by the BMW 320i.

THE BMW 320i VS. UNREASONABLE FACSIMILES.

The 320i is engineered according to a belief that hasn't changed for decades:

Namely, that performance is, and will always be, the ultimate measure of a car's worth—a belief that permits a car to grow by gradual refinement, instead of hasty responses to the caprices of fashion.

The current preference for leaner, more efficient engines, for example, has caused no radical reshuffling of priorities at BMW. The 320i is powered by a 1.8-liter engine equipped with K-Jetronic fuel injection—and has been for years, before the industry at large discovered the superiority of such a system.

Nor has the 320i needed any instant re-engineering to deliver better mileage. It delivers an EPA-estimated [25] mpg, 36 mpg highway, figures that would be respectable even in an economy car.

(Fuel efficiency figures are for comparison purposes only. Your actual mileage may vary, depending on speed, weather and trip length. Your actual highway mileage will most likely be lower.)

And while many cars are rediscovering the driver as an integral part of the car, no such rediscovery was necessary in the 320i.

Everything in its interior is designed to encourage maximum performance in both driver and automobile. Including controls and instrumentation that are easily readable and reachable; and seats orthopedically designed to reduce driver fatigue.

In fact, despite all the flurry of emulation, the 320i—with its fully independent suspension, precise steering, and decades of technological refinements bred on racecourses—remains uniquely driveable.

So much so as to awaken an almost unseemly ardor in automotive critics who are implacable for a living.

One nominates the 320i as "the sort of car enthusiasts turn into legend." He might have added that there are no reasonable facsimiles for legends.

INVEST IN AN ORIGINAL INSTEAD OF A REPRODUCTION.

Originals generally bring their owners higher prices than reproductions. Which could help account for the following:

According to the January 1981 NADA Used-Car Guide, while the value of other cars was dwindling considerably, the average 320i sold over the past 4 years retained a phenomenal 95.2% of its original price.

All things considered, the appearance of so many BMW surrogates is perfectly understandable.

If you suspect you might not be content to spend the next several years with a surrogate, we suggest you contact your nearest BMW dealer for a test drive.

THE ULTIMATE DRIVING MACHINE.
BMW, MUNICH, GERMANY

©1981 BMW of North America, Inc. The BMW trademark and logo are registered trademarks of Bayerische Motoren Werke, A.G.

1982

ART DIRECTOR
Anthony Angotti

WRITER
Tom Thomas

DESIGNERS
Barbara Sharman
Barbara Bowman
Denise Monaco
Dominique Singer

PHOTOGRAPHER
Dick James

CLIENT
BMW of North America

AGENCY
Ammirati & Puris

1985
ART DIRECTOR
Gary Johns
WRITER
Jeff Gorman
CLIENT
Nike
AGENCY
Chiat/Day - Los Angeles

STATISTICS FOR PEOPLE INTERESTED IN NOT BECOMING STATISTICS.

"A barrier impact at 35 mph can generate between 80,000 and 120,000 lbs of force."

"In a 30 mph front end collision, a 165 lb man hits the windshield with a force of 3 tons."

"A 10 mph increase in impact speed from 30 to 40 mph means that 79% more energy must be absorbed."

Let a bunch of safety engineers slam enough cars into a wall and statistics like these begin to pile up.

The more of them you have to work with, the safer the car you can build.

At Volvo, safety has always been a high priority.

So every year at our Technical Center in Gothenburg, Sweden, we destroy between 70 and 80 Volvos in crash tests. And the statistics we've gathered over the years have helped us make the kinds of innovations that have made Volvo the standard of safety for the automobile industry.

Our now famous steel "safety cage," for instance, surrounds the passenger compartment of a Volvo and is designed to keep it from crumpling during a collision. Every weld in it is strong enough to support the weight of the entire car.

At either end of a Volvo is a built-in safety zone. It's especially designed *to* crumple in order to absorb some of the energy forces of a collision instead of passing them along to the occupants.

To make sure you have protection on all sides in a Volvo, we've placed tubular, steel anti-intrusion bars in all doors.

Even our steering column is designed to collapse upon impact and our laminated windshield is designed to remain intact.

Of course no car can protect you in a crash unless you're wearing the safety innovation that became standard equipment in Volvos back in 1959: the three point safety belt. (Statistics show that fifty percent of the deaths due to road accidents could be avoided if drivers and passengers were wearing them.)

So if you're interested in not becoming a highway statistic, take a precaution the next time you take to the highway.

Be sure to fasten your safety belt.

And incidentally, it might be a good idea to be sure it's fastened to a Volvo.

VOLVO
A car you can believe in.

1985

ART DIRECTOR
Simon Bowden

WRITER
Frank Fleizach

PHOTOGRAPHER
Harry DeZitter

CLIENT
Volvo

AGENCY
Scali McCabe Sloves

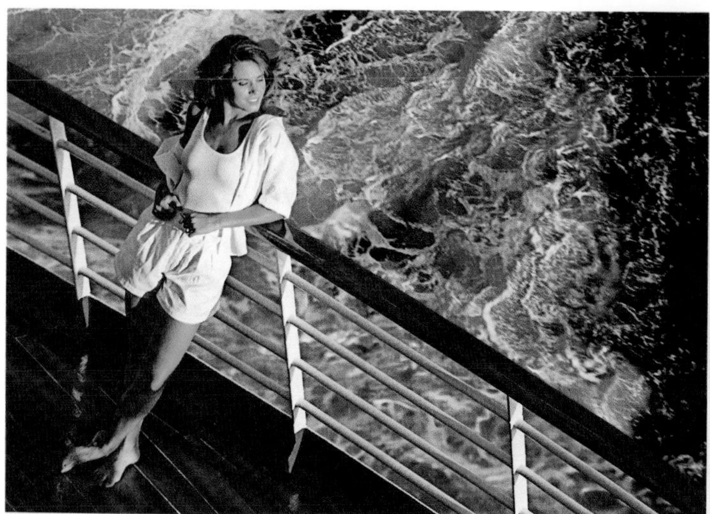

The water slides by in blue-white ripples, punctuated now and then by the leap of a flying fish.

The breeze, as it skims past you down the open deck, seems to carry all your worries right out to sea.

And the sun, high in a tropical sky, warms parts of your psyche you didn't even know were cold.

On a Royal Caribbean cruise, you can leave the pressures behind.

And renew the energies sapped by all those years of full-speed-ahead.

We'll take you to mountains that rise out of turquoise seas, only to lose themselves in layers of cloud.

To fortifications once guarded by the Conquistadores. To old churches whose mosaics arch toward vaulted stone ceilings. To islands where the beaches stretch for miles.

We'll cater to your taste for good food and good company. Entertain you. Indulge you. Totally spoil you. For seven, eight, ten or fourteen days.

Just see your travel agent about a Royal Caribbean cruise.

It may be exactly what you need to get yourself in high gear again.

ROYAL CARIBBEAN

Song of Norway, Song of America, Nordic Prince, Sun Viking
Ships of Norwegian Registry

Our Ships Don't Have Sails, But They Could Put The Wind Back Into Yours.

The decks are strung with lights that soar high above the sea, framing the deepening indigo of the night.

Far below you, on the water, the reflection of a tropical moon scatters into a thousand glowing bits.

When evening comes, on a Royal Caribbean cruise, you'll see that all the romantic stories you've heard about cruising are absolutely true.

You'll sip a vintage Bordeaux, savor a perfectly prepared leg of lamb, indulge yourself in Cherries Jubilee flamed right at your table.

You'll watch the silent passing of a freighter, far out on the horizon. And dance under more stars than you ever thought the sky could hold.

And you'll find that the warmth of the islands lingers in your mind, long after the sun goes down.

So talk to your travel agent about a Royal Caribbean cruise. For seven, eight, ten or fourteen days.

After all, some things are just too good to be left to your imagination.

ROYAL CARIBBEAN

Song of Norway, Song of America, Nordic Prince, Sun Viking
Ships of Norwegian Registry

Now Imagine The Same Idea, On A Slightly Larger Scale.

Somewhere, deep in your mind, is a child who grew up with dreams of adventure and romance.

A child who could turn a toy boat into a sailing ship. And a bathtub into the bounding main.

On a Royal Caribbean cruise, you could find yourself getting to know that child all over again.

You could spend seven, eight, ten, or even fourteen days discovering storybook islands ringed with palm trees and scented with hibiscus.

You could dance to the pulsating rhythm of steel drums. Dine on fresh pineapple and flaming babalu. Meet a neon-blue fish, face to face, in the lacy shadows of a coral reef.

Or stand high on a polished deck, with a warm breeze in your face, as your ship glides through an indigo sea that stretches all the way to the edges of your imagination.

Just see your travel agent about a Royal Caribbean cruise.

It can take you away to some of the most beautiful places on earth.

And take you back to some of the most beautiful times of your life.

ROYAL CARIBBEAN

Song of Norway, Song of America, Nordic Prince, Sun Viking
Ships of Norwegian Registry

Ever Since You Were A Kid, You've Wanted To Take A Cruise.

1986

ART DIRECTOR
Larry Bennett

WRITER
Harriet Frye

PHOTOGRAPHERS
Barbara Bordnick
Tim Olive

CLIENT
Royal Caribbean Cruise Line

AGENCY
McKinney Silver &
Rockett/Raleigh, NC

In North Carolina, some of our greatest works of art never hang in a museum.

Dove-In-The-Window. Star of Bethlehem. Wild Goose Chase. Wedding Ring.

High in the North Carolina mountains, quilts are made to be purely practical. Yet their ageless patterns make them purely beautiful. Quilts, however, are just one expression of our highland artistry.

Some people can put their penknife to a block of sugar maple and magically reveal the form of a wild turkey or a good hunting dog.

Others make sturdy pots with glazes as guardedly secret as prized family recipes.

And still others display their art in jars of jam and jelly, or in jugs of amber apple cider found at roadside stands.

Wherever you travel, from our mountains to our shore, you'll be certain to find art that exhibits itself proudly.

So, if you're the kind of person who appreciates finer things, you really don't have to visit the museums.

Come to North Carolina, and visit us instead.

For our new travel package, just write NC Travel, Dept. 589, Raleigh, NC 27699. Or, in Michigan, Ohio, Illinois and Indiana, call (weekdays 8 a.m.–5 p.m.): 1-800-VISIT NC, Operator 589.

North Carolina

If you are what you eat, a visit to North Carolina could make you a very interesting person, indeed.

Grits Souffle. Squash Pie. Wild Persimmon Pudding. Chow Chow. Corn Dodgers.

Across the gently rolling midlands of North Carolina, what we eat is hardly the same old blue plate special.

To family reunions and church dinners across the state, we bring dishes like our Green Tomato Pie and Pig Pickin' Cake, which puzzle the uninitiated and thoroughly delight the oldtimers.

But you don't have to call North Carolina home just to sample our great homecooking.

Because we also cook like this away from home.

Which means you'll find these interesting dishes in small cafes and old inns, when you travel from our Blue Ridge mountains to our shore.

So, come. Because a visit to North Carolina is more than food for the appetite.

It's also food for the soul.

For our new travel package, write North Carolina Travel, Dept. 457, Raleigh, NC 27699. Or call 1-800-VISIT NC, Operator 457.

North Carolina

Our cruise lines may not be known for elegant dining, but they'll take you to some beautiful islands.

Drive to the bank of the Cashie River in North Carolina, and honk the horn. And when the ferry chugs over to pick you up, you can cruise to the other side. Free.

Or, you can take a ferry to faraway places with strange-sounding names like Hatteras, Ocracoke, and Rodanthe.

Several of these rugged barrier islands are so remote, the people speak a foreign language: Olde English. And some are so unspoiled, you can still see the same pristine beauty that enchanted our first settlers from Wales, Scotland and England.

Whether you explore 25 miles of national seashore or visit our colorful fishing villages, you'll discover this:

Our cruise lines may not offer elegant dining.

But they can help satisfy your appetite for adventure.

For our new travel package, write North Carolina Travel, Dept. 466, Raleigh, NC 27699. Or call 1-800-VISIT NC, Operator 466.

North Carolina

1987

ART DIRECTORS
Michael Winslow
Mark Oakley

WRITER
Jan Karon

PHOTOGRAPHER
Harry DeZitter

CLIENT
North Carolina Travel and Tourism

AGENCY
McKinney & Silver/
Raleigh, NC

Tip O'Neill. Cardmember since 1973.

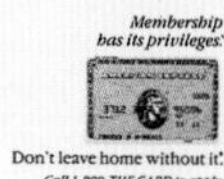

Wilt Chamberlain. Cardmember since 1976.
Willie Shoemaker. Cardmember since 1966.

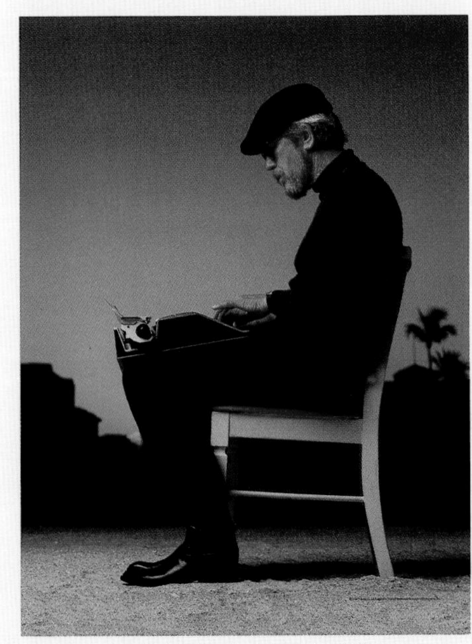

Elmore Leonard. Cardmember since 1961.

1988

ART DIRECTOR
Parry Merkley

WRITER
Gordon Bowen

PHOTOGRAPHER
Annie Leibovitz

CLIENT
American Express

AGENCY
Ogilvy & Mather

Life Is Two Periods Of Play Interrupted By Forty Years Of Work.

Our days on this earth are too precious to spend any more of them doing things you don't want to do.

So welcome back to the World of Play: a world where you again have the time and freedom to do whatever you please. Driving. Walking. Swimming, fishing, biking. Spelunking. Just plain exploring.

To help you in your new adventure, we make Itasca® motor homes. Think of an Itasca as the home for your second childhood. And the world is your backyard.

Put yourself in an Itasca. Get way, way out there. Chase some horizons. And do something befitting a person of your rank and stature.

Go fly a kite.

Itasca® The Road To A Fuller Life.

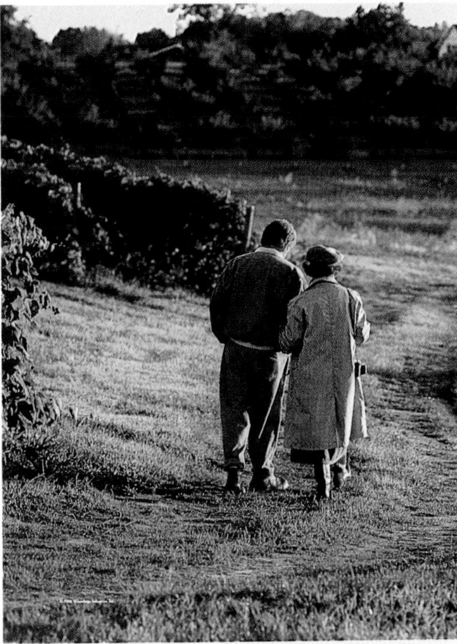

Isn't It About Time You Got To Know The Person You've Spent Your Life With?

It seems forever ago; it seems like yesterday. You met. Courted. Married. Then, some time, it stopped being just the two of you. Children and careers intervened. Business trips. Chicken pox. Saturdays at the office. The mumps.

Now, almost suddenly, it's just the two of you again. Two people who, in many ways, have been given the chance to start all over again.

To help make your new relationship a satisfying one, we bring you Itasca® motor homes. Let an Itasca be the vehicle for your second courtship. Who knows? It could be even better than the first.

You know each other a little better now. The awkwardness of youth is gone.

And this time around, your date doesn't have a curfew.

Itasca® The Road To A Fuller Life.

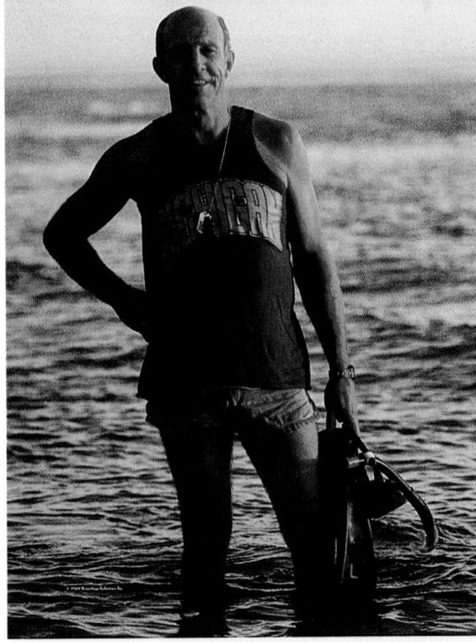

What's The Use Of Living To A Ripe Old Age If You're Just Going To Sit Around Getting Soft?

Chances are, when you were a kid, you made a secret list of things you wanted to do in life. Mountains you wanted to climb. Pearls you wanted to dive for. Instruments you wanted to make sing.

Then "reality" (adulthood) set in, and those dreams were put on hold.

At Itasca® motor homes, we specialize in helping people dust off those dreams and finally do something about them. An Itasca gives you the freedom to get right out there and do it — whatever "it" may be.

So c'mon. Get moving. Throw away the cheese puffs, and march out into the world of dreams fulfilled.

In other words: Take a hike.

Itasca® The Road To A Fuller Life.

1989
ART DIRECTOR
Jim Keane
WRITER
Phil Calvit
PHOTOGRAPHER
Tom Berthiaume
CLIENT
Itasca Motor Home
AGENCY
Carmichael Lynch/
Minneapolis

Or buy a Volkswagen.

Volkswagen makes the 3 highest mileage cars in America: the Rabbit Diesel 5-speed, Rabbit Diesel 4-speed and the Dasher Diesels.
Rabbit Diesel 5-speed, est [41] mpg. 55 mpg est hwy Rabbit Diesel 4-speed, est [40] mpg. 50 mpg est hwy Dasher Diesels, est [36] mpg. 46 mpg est hwy.
(Compare these EPA est to the est mpg of other cars. Your mileage may vary with speed, weather and trip length. Hwy mileage will probably be less.)

1980

ART DIRECTOR
Charles Piccirillo

WRITER
Robert Levenson

ARTIST
Charles Piccirillo

CLIENT
Volkswagen

AGENCY
Doyle Dane Bernbach

How to write clearly

By Edward T. Thompson
Editor-in-Chief, Reader's Digest

International Paper asked Edward T. Thompson to share some of what he has learned in nineteen years with Reader's Digest, a magazine famous for making complicated subjects understandable to millions of readers.

If you are afraid to write, don't be.

If you think you've got to string together big fancy words and high-flying phrases, forget it.

To write well, unless you aspire to be a professional poet or novelist, you only need to get your ideas across simply and clearly.

It's not easy. But it *is* easier than you might imagine.

There are only three basic requirements:

First, you must *want* to write clearly. And I believe you really do, if you've stayed this far with me.

Second, you must be willing to *work hard*. Thinking means work—and that's what it takes to do anything well.

Third, you must know and follow some *basic guidelines*.

If, while you're writing for clarity, some lovely, dramatic or inspired phrases or sentences come to you, fine. Put them in.

But then with cold, objective eyes and mind ask yourself: "Do they detract from clarity?" If they do, grit your teeth and cut the frills.

Follow some basic guidelines

I can't give you a complete list of "dos and don'ts" for every writing problem you'll ever face.

But I can give you some fundamental guidelines that cover the most common problems.

1. Outline what you want to say.

I know that sounds grade-schoolish. But you can't write clearly until, *before you start*, you know where you will stop.

Ironically, that's even a problem in writing an outline (i.e., knowing the ending before you begin).

So try this method:

- On 3"x 5" cards, write—one point to a card—all the points you need to make.
- Divide the cards into piles—one pile for each group of points *closely related* to each other. (If you were describing an automobile, you'd put all the points about mileage in one pile, all the points about safety in another, and so on.)
- Arrange your piles of points in a sequence. Which are most important and should be given first or saved for last? Which must you present before others in order to make the others understandable?
- Now, *within* each pile, do the same thing—arrange the *points* in logical, understandable order.

There you have your outline, needing only an introduction and conclusion.

This is a practical way to outline. It's also flexible. You can add, delete or change the location of points easily.

2. Start where your readers are.

How much do they know about the subject? Don't write to a level higher than your readers' knowledge of it.

CAUTION: Forget that old—and wrong—advice about writing to a 12-year-old mentality. That's insulting. But do remember that your prime purpose is to *explain* something, not prove that you're smarter than your readers.

3. Avoid jargon.

Don't use words, expressions, phrases known only to people with specific knowledge or interests.

Example: A scientist, using scientific jargon, wrote, "The biota exhibited a one hundred percent mortality response." He could have written: "All the fish died."

4. Use familiar combinations of words.

A speech writer for President Franklin D. Roosevelt wrote, "We are endeavoring to construct a more inclusive society." F.D.R. changed it to, "We're going to make a country in which no one is left out."

CAUTION: By familiar combinations of words, I do *not* mean incorrect grammar. *That* can be *un*clear. Example: John's father says he can't go out Friday. (Who can't go out? John or his father?)

5. Use "first-degree" words.

These words immediately bring an image to your mind. Other words must be "translated" through the first-degree word before you see the image. Those are second/third-degree words.

First-degree words	Second/third-degree words
face	visage, countenance
stay	abide, remain, reside
book	volume, tome, publication

"Outline for clarity. Write your points on 3"x 5" cards—one point to a card. Then you can easily add to, or change the order of points—even delete some."

First-degree words are usually the most precise words, too.

6. Stick to the point.

Your outline— which was more work in the beginning—now saves you work. Because now you can ask about any sentence you write: "Does it relate to a point in the outline? If it doesn't, should I add it to the outline? If not, I'm getting off the track." Then, full steam ahead—on the main line.

7. Be as brief as possible.

Whatever you write, shortening—*condensing*—almost always makes it tighter, straighter, easier to read and understand.

Condensing, as *Reader's Digest* does it, is in large part artistry. But it involves techniques that anyone can learn and use.

- *Present your points in logical ABC order:* Here again, your outline should save you work because, if you did it right, your points already stand in logical ABC order—A makes B understandable, B makes C understandable and so on. To write in a straight line is to say something clearly in the fewest possible words.
- *Don't waste words telling people what they already know:* Notice how we edited this: "Have you ever wondered how banks rate you as a credit risk? ~~You know, of course, that it's some combination of facts about your income, your job, and so on. But actually,~~ Many banks have a scoring system…."
- *Cut out excess evidence and unnecessary anecdotes:* Usually, one fact or example (at most, two) will support a point. More just belabor it. And while writing about something may remind you of a good story, ask yourself: "Does it *really help* to tell the story, or does it slow me down?"

(Many people think *Reader's Digest* articles are filled with anecdotes. Actually, we use them sparingly and usually for one of two reasons: either the subject is so dry it needs some "humanity" to give it life; or the subject is so hard to grasp, it needs anecdotes to help readers understand. If the subject is both lively and easy to grasp, we move right along.)

- *Look for the most common word wasters:* windy phrases.

Windy phrases	Cut to…
at the present time	now
in the event of	if
in the majority of instances	usually

- *Look for passive verbs you can make active:* Invariably, this produces a shorter sentence. "The cherry tree *was* chopped down by George Washington." (Passive verb and nine words.) "George Washington *chopped* down the cherry tree." (Active verb and seven words.)
- *Look for positive/negative sections from which you can cut the negative:* See how we did it here: "The answer ~~does not rest with carelessness or incompetence. It lies largely in~~ is having enough people to do the job."
- Finally, to write more clearly by saying it in fewer words: when you've finished, stop.

"Grit your teeth and cut the frills. That's one of the suggestions I offer here to help you write clearly. They cover the most common problems. And they're all easy to follow."

The biota exhibited a 100% mortality response

Writing clearly means avoiding jargon. Why didn't he just say: "All the fish died!"

Edward T. Thompson

Today, the printed word is more vital than ever. Now there is more need than ever for all of us to *read* better, *write* better, and *communicate* better.

International Paper offers this series in the hope that, even in a small way, we can help.

If you'd like to share this article with others—students, friends, employees, family—we'll gladly send you reprints. So far we've sent out over 15,000,000 in response to requests from people everywhere.

Please write: "Power of the Printed Word," International Paper Company, Dept. 4H, P.O. Box 954, Madison Square Station, New York, NY 10010.

INTERNATIONAL PAPER COMPANY
We believe in the power of the printed word.

How to read faster

By Bill Cosby

International Paper asked Bill Cosby—who earned his doctorate in education and has been involved in projects which help people learn to read faster—to share what he's learned about reading more in less time.

When I was a kid in Philadelphia, I must have read every comic book ever published. (There were fewer of them then than there are now.)

I zipped through all of them in a couple of days, then reread the good ones until the next issues arrived.

Yes indeed, when I was a kid, the reading game was a snap.

But as I got older, my eyeballs must have slowed down or something! I mean, comic books started to pile up faster than my brother Russell and I could read them!

It wasn't until much later, when I was getting my doctorate, I realized it wasn't my eyeballs that were to blame. Thank goodness. They're still moving as well as ever.

The problem is, there's too much to read these days, and too little time to read every word of it.

Now, mind you, I still read comic books. In addition to contracts, novels, and newspapers. Screenplays, tax returns and correspondence. Even textbooks about how people read. And which techniques help people read more in less time.

I'll let you in on a little secret. There are hundreds of techniques you could learn to help you read faster. But I know of 3 that are especially good.

And if I can learn them, so can you—and you can put them to use *immediately*.

They are commonsense, practical ways to get the meaning from printed words quickly and efficiently. So you'll have time to enjoy your comic books, have a good laugh with Mark Twain or a good cry with *War and Peace*. Ready?

Okay. The first two ways can help you get through tons of reading material—fast—*without reading every word*.

They'll give you the *overall meaning* of what you're reading. And let you cut out an awful lot of *unnecessary* reading.

1. Preview—if it's long and hard

Previewing is especially useful for getting a general idea of heavy reading like long magazine or newspaper articles, business reports, and nonfiction books.

It can give you as much as half the comprehension in as little as one tenth the time. For example, you should be able to preview eight or ten 100-page reports in an hour. After previewing, you'll be able to decide which reports (or which *parts* of which reports) are worth a closer look.

Here's how to preview: Read the entire first two paragraphs of whatever you've chosen. Next read only the *first sentence* of each successive paragraph. Then read the entire last two paragraphs.

Previewing doesn't give you all the details. But it does keep you from spending time on things you don't really want—or need—to read.

Notice that previewing gives you a quick, overall view of *long, unfamiliar* material. For short, light reading, there's a better technique.

2. Skim—if it's short and simple

Skimming is a good way to get a general idea of light reading—like popular magazines or the sports and entertainment sections of the paper.

You should be able to skim a weekly popular magazine or the second section of your daily paper in less than *half* the time it takes you to read it now.

Skimming is also a great way to review material you've read before.

Here's how to skim: Think of your eyes as magnets. Force them to move fast. Sweep them across each and every line of type. Pick up *only a few key words in each line*.

Everybody skims differently.

You and I may not pick up exactly the same words when we skim the same piece, but we'll both get a pretty similar idea of what it's all about.

To show you how it works, I circled the words I picked out when I skimmed the following story. Try it. It shouldn't take you more than 10 seconds.

My brother Russell thinks monsters live in our bedroom closet at night. But I told him he is crazy.

"Go and check then," he said.

I didn't want to. Russell said I was chicken.

"Am not," I said.

"Are so," he said.

So I told him the monsters were going to eat him at midnight. He started to cry. My Dad came in and told the monsters to beat it. Then he told us to go to sleep.

"If I hear any more about monsters," he said, "I'll spank you."

We went to sleep fast. And you know something? They never did come back.

"Learn to read faster and you'll have time for a good laugh with Mark Twain—and a good cry with War and Peace."

Skimming can give you a very good *idea* of this story in about half the words—and in *less* than half the time it'd take to read every word.

So far, you've seen that previewing and skimming can give you a *general idea* about content—fast. But neither technique can promise more than 50 percent comprehension, because you aren't reading all the words. (Nobody gets something for nothing in the reading game.)

To *read faster and understand most*—if not all—of what you read, you need to know a third technique.

"Read with a good light—and with as few friends as possible to help you out. No TV, no music. It'll help you concentrate better—and read faster."

3. Cluster—to increase speed and comprehension

Most of us learned to read by looking at each word in a sentence—*one at a time*.

Like this:

My—brother—Russell—thinks—monsters…

You probably still read this way sometimes, especially when the words are difficult. Or when the words have an extra-special meaning—as in a poem, a Shakespearean play, or a contract. And that's O.K.

But word-by-word reading is a rotten way to read faster. It actually *cuts down* on your speed.

Clustering trains you to look at *groups* of words instead of one at a time—to increase your speed enormously. For most of us, clustering is a *totally different way of seeing what we read*.

Here's how to cluster: Train your eyes to see *all* the words in clusters of up to 3 or 4 words at a glance.

Here's how I'd cluster the story we just skimmed:

My brother Russell thinks monsters live in our bedroom closet at night. But I told him he is crazy.

"Go and check then," he said.

I didn't want to. Russell said I was chicken.

"Am not," I said.

"Are so," he said.

So I told him the monsters were going to eat him at midnight. He started to cry. My Dad came in and told the monsters to beat it. Then he told us to go to sleep.

"If I hear any more about monsters," he said, "I'll spank you."

We went to sleep fast. And you know something? They never did come back.

Learning to read clusters is not something your eyes do naturally. It takes constant practice.

Here's how to go about it: Pick something light to read. Read it as fast as you can. Concentrate on seeing 3 to 4 words at once rather than one word at a time. Then reread the piece at your normal speed to see what you missed the first time.

Try a second piece. First cluster, then reread to see what you missed in this one.

When you can read in clusters without missing much the first time, your speed has increased. Practice 15 minutes every day and you might pick up the technique in a week or so. (But don't be disappointed if it takes longer. Clustering *everything* takes time and practice.)

So now you have 3 ways to help you read faster. Preview to cut down on unnecessary heavy reading. Skim to get a quick, general idea of light reading. And cluster to increase your speed *and* comprehension.

With enough practice, you'll be able to handle *more* reading at school or work—and at home—*in less time*. You should even have enough time to read your favorite comic books—and *War and Peace*!

"Preview, skim, and cluster to read faster—except the things you want to read word for word."

Bill Cosby

Today, the printed word is more vital than ever. Now there is more need than ever for all of us to *read* better, *write* better, and *communicate* better.

International Paper offers this series in the hope that, even in a small way, we can help.

If you'd like to share this article with others—students, friends, employees, family—we'll gladly send you reprints. So far we've sent out over 14,000,000 in response to requests from people everywhere.

Please write: "Power of the Printed Word," International Paper Company, Dept. 3X, P.O. Box 954, Madison Square Station, New York, NY 10010.

INTERNATIONAL PAPER COMPANY
We believe in the power of the printed word.

How to improve your vocabulary

By Tony Randall

International Paper asked Tony Randall—who is on The American Heritage Dictionary Usage Panel, and loves words almost as much as acting—to tell how he has acquired his enormous vocabulary.

Words can make us laugh, cry, go to war, fall in love.

Rudyard Kipling called words the most powerful drug of mankind. If they are, I'm a hopeless addict—and I hope to get you hooked, too!

Whether you're still in school or you head up a corporation, the better command you have of words, the better chance you have of saying exactly what you mean, of understanding what others mean—and of getting what you want in the world.

English is the richest language—with the largest vocabulary on earth. Over 1,000,000 words!

You can express shades of meaning that aren't even *possible* in other languages. (For example, you can differentiate between "sky" and "heaven." The French, Italians and Spanish cannot.)

Yet, the average adult has a vocabulary of only 30,000 to 60,000 words. Imagine what we're missing!

Here are five pointers that help me learn—and remember—whole *families* of words at a time.

They may not *look* easy—and won't be at first. But if you stick with them you'll find they *work!*

What's the first thing to do when you see a word you don't know?

1. Try to guess the meaning of the word from the way it's used

You can often get at least *part* of a word's meaning—just from how it's used in a sentence.

That's why it's so important to read as much as you can—different *kinds* of things: magazines, books, newspapers you don't normally read. The more you *expose* yourself to new words, the more words you'll pick up *just by seeing how they're used.*

For instance, say you run across the word "manacle":

> "The manacles had been on John's wrists for 30 years. Only one person had a key—his wife."

You have a good *idea* of what "manacles" are—just from the context of the sentence.

But let's find out *exactly* what the word means and where it comes from. The only way to do this, and to build an extensive vocabulary *fast*, is to go to the dictionary. (How lucky, you *can*—Shakespeare *couldn't*. There *wasn't* an English dictionary in his day!)

So you go to the dictionary. (NOTE: Don't let dictionary abbreviations put you off. The front tells you what they mean, and even has a guide to pronunciation.)

2. Look it up

Here's the definition for "manacle" in *The American Heritage Dictionary of the English Language.*

man-a-cle (măn'ə-kəl) n. Usually plural. **1.** A device for confining the hands, usually consisting of two metal rings that are fastened about the wrists and joined by a metal chain; a handcuff. **2.** Anything that confines or restrains.—tr.v. **manacled, -cling, -cles. 1.** To restrain with manacles. **2.** To confine or restrain as if with manacles; shackle; fetter. [Middle English *manicle*, from Old French, from Latin *manicula*, little hand, handle, diminutive of *manus*, hand. See **man-**[2] in Appendix.*]

The first definition fits here: A device for confining the hands, usually consisting of two metal rings that are fastened about the wrists and joined by a metal chain; a handcuff.

Well, that's what you *thought* it meant. But what's the idea *behind* the word? What are its *roots*? To really understand a word, you need to know.

Here's where the detective work—and the *fun*—begins.

3. Dig the meaning out by the roots

The root is the basic part of the word—its heritage, its origin. (Most of our roots come from Latin and Greek words at least 2,000 years old—which come from even earlier Indo-European tongues!)

"'Emancipate' has a Latin root. Learn it and you'll know other words at a glance."

Learning the roots: 1) Helps us *remember* words. 2) Gives us a deeper understanding of the words we *already* know. And 3) allows us to pick up whole families of *new* words at a time. That's why learning the root is the *most important part of going to the dictionary.*

Notice the root of "manacle" is *manus* (Latin) meaning "hand."

Well, that makes sense. Now, other words with this root, man, start to make sense, too.

Take manual—something done "by hand" (manual labor) or a "handbook." And manage—to "handle" something (as a manager). When you emancipate someone, you're taking him "from the hands of" someone else.

When you manufacture something, you "make it by hand" (in its original meaning).

And when you finish your first novel, your publisher will see your—originally "handwritten"—manuscript.

Imagine! A whole new world of words opens up—just from one simple root!

The root gives the *basic* clue to the meaning of a word. But there's another important clue that runs a close second—the *prefix*.

"Your main clue to remembering a word is its root—its origin."

4. Get the powerful prefixes under your belt

A prefix is the part that's sometimes attached to the front of a word. Like—well, *prefix!* There aren't many—less than 100 major prefixes—and you'll learn them in no time at all just by becoming more aware of the meanings of words you already know. Here are a few. (Some of the "How-to" vocabulary-building books will give you the others.)

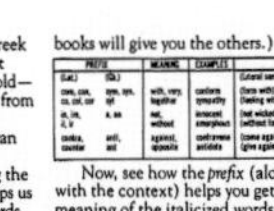

PREFIX (Lat.)	PREFIX (Gr.)	MEANING	EXAMPLES	(Literal sense)
com, con, co, col, cor	syn, sym, syl	with, very, together	conform, sympathy	(form with), (feeling with)
in, im, il, ir	a, an	not, without	innocent, amorphous	(not wicked), (without form)
contra, counter	anti, ant	against, opposite	contravene, antidote	(come against), (give against)

Now, see how the *prefix* (along with the context) helps you get the meaning of the italicized words:

- "If you're going to be my witness, your story must *corroborate* my story." (The literal meaning of *corroborate* is "strength together.")
- "You told me one thing—now you tell me another. Don't *contradict* yourself." (The literal meaning of *contradict* is "say against.")
- "Oh, that snake's not poisonous. It's a completely *innocuous* little garden snake." (The literal meaning of *innocuous* is "not harmful.")

Now, you've got some new words. What are you going to do with them?

5. Put your new words to work at once

Use them several times the first day you learn them. Say them out loud! Write them in sentences.

Should you "use" them on *friends*? Careful—you don't wan them to think you're a stuffed shirt. (It depends on the situation. You *know* when a word sounds natural—and when it sounds stuffy.)

How about your *enemies*? You have my blessing. Ask one of them if he's read that article on pneumonoultramicroscopicsilicovolcanoconiosis. (You really can find it in the dictionary.) Now, you're one up on him.

So what do you do to improve your vocabulary?

Remember: 1) Try to guess the meaning of the word from the way it's used. 2) Look it up. 3) Dig the meaning out by the roots. 4) Get the powerful prefixes under your belt. 5) Put your new words to work at once.

That's all there is to it—you're off on your treasure hunt.

Now, do you see why I love words so much?

Aristophanes said, "By words, the mind is excited and the spirit elated." It's as true today as it was when he said it in Athens—2,400 *years ago!*

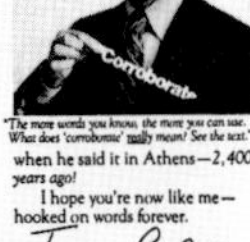

"The more words you know, the more you can use. What does 'corroborate' really mean? See the text."

I hope you're now like me—hooked on words forever.

Tony Randall

Years ago, International Paper sponsored a series of advertisements, "Send me a man who reads," to help make Americans more aware of the value of reading.

Today, the printed word is more vital than ever. Now there is more need than ever before for all of us to *read* better, *write* better, and *communicate* better.

International Paper offers this *new* series in the hope that, even in a small way, we can help.

For reprints of this advertisement, write: "Power of the Printed Word," International Paper Co., Dept. 2-B, P.O. Box 900, Elmsford, New York 10523.

INTERNATIONAL PAPER COMPANY
We believe in the power of the printed word.

1980

ART DIRECTOR
Herb Jager

WRITER
Billings Fuess

DESIGNER
Herb Jager

ARTIST
Arnie Levin

PHOTOGRAPHERS
Harold Krieger
John Cahoon

CLIENT
International Paper

AGENCY
Ogilvy & Mather

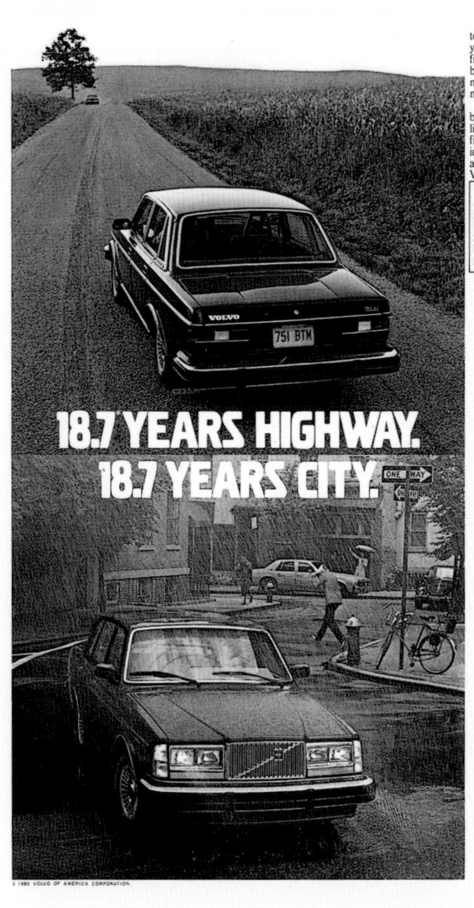

A lot of car makers today are trying to sell you economy with EPA figures. But at Volvo, we believe true economy isn't more miles per gallon. It's more years per car.

So if you just want to buy less gas and save a little money, look at EPA figures. But if you like the idea of buying fewer cars and saving a lot, consider Volvo's figures.

***Average life expectancy of a Volvo in Sweden. Driving conditions in the United States may differ. So your Volvo may not last as long. Then again, it may last longer.**

VOLVO
A car you can believe in.

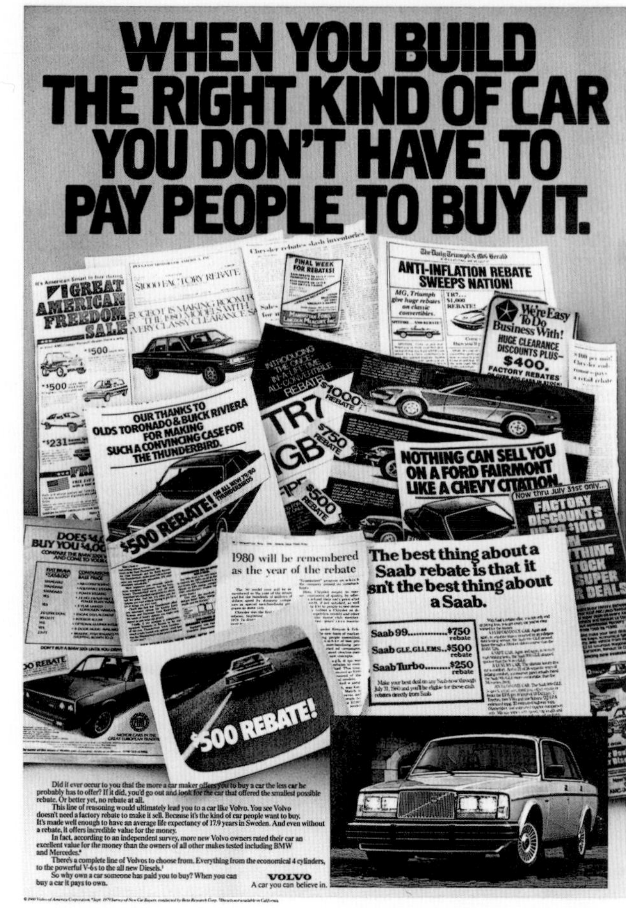

"ANYONE WHO'S THINKING OF SPENDING $24,000 FOR A LUXURY CAR SHOULD TALK TO A PSYCHIATRIST."

—Dr. John Boston, psychiatrist and Volvo owner, Austin, Texas

John Boston, a Texas psychiatrist, owns a '73 Volvo.

He bought that Volvo because, as he puts it: "I had admired what Volvo had done in the area of safety. The car seemed well-built. It offered solid European craftsmanship without the inflated price."

We wanted Dr. Boston's opinion of the new Volvo GLE, which has a full assortment of luxury features as standard equipment—and a price tag thousands of dollars below that of the well-known German luxury sedan.

"It's an excellent value. In my opinion, the individual buying this car would have a strong, unsuppressed need to get his or her money's worth. He or she would probably also have a strong enough self-image not to need a blatant status symbol."

When we told him that some people were actually paying five to ten thousand dollars more for a luxury car, Dr. Boston's response was characteristically succinct.

"That's not using your head."

Finally, we asked Dr. Boston if, when he was ready for a new car, he'd consider the Volvo GLE for himself.

"I'd be crazy if I didn't."

VOLVO
A car you can believe in.

1981

ART DIRECTOR
Jim Perretti

WRITERS
Frank Fleizach
Larry Cadman

DESIGNER
Jim Perretti

PHOTOGRAPHER
Phil Mazzurco

CLIENT
Volvo

AGENCY
Scali McCabe Sloves

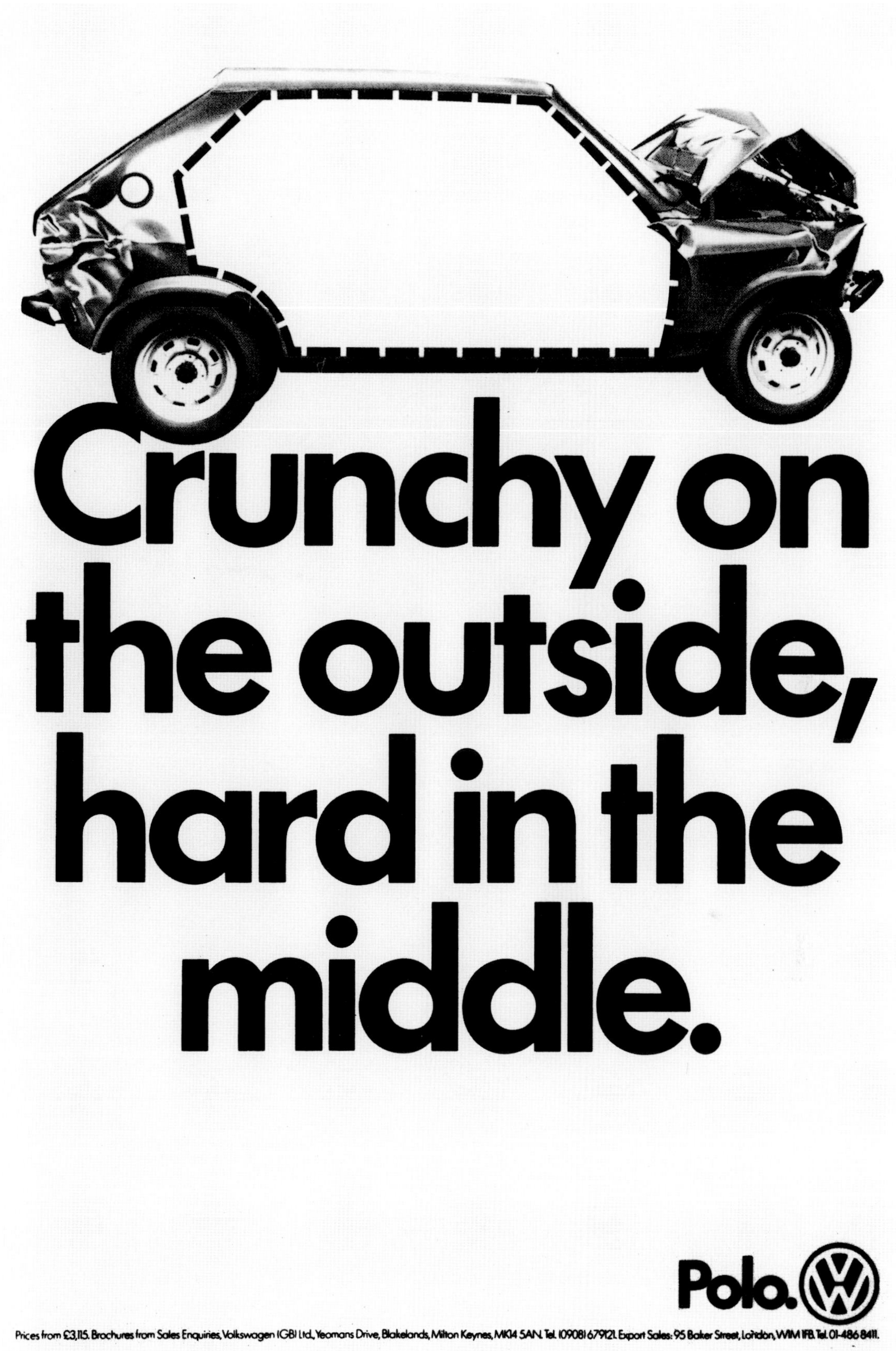

Crunchy on the outside, hard in the middle.

Prices from £3,115. Brochures from Sales Enquiries, Volkswagen (GB) Ltd., Yeomans Drive, Blakelands, Milton Keynes, MK14 5AN. Tel. (0908) 679121. Export Sales: 95 Baker Street, London, W1M 1FB. Tel. 01-486 8411.

1981

ART DIRECTORS
Max Henry
Peter Harold

WRITER
Barbara Nokes

DESIGNER
Max Henry

PHOTOGRAPHER
Geoff Senior

CLIENT
Volkswagen

AGENCY
Doyle Dane Bernbach/
London

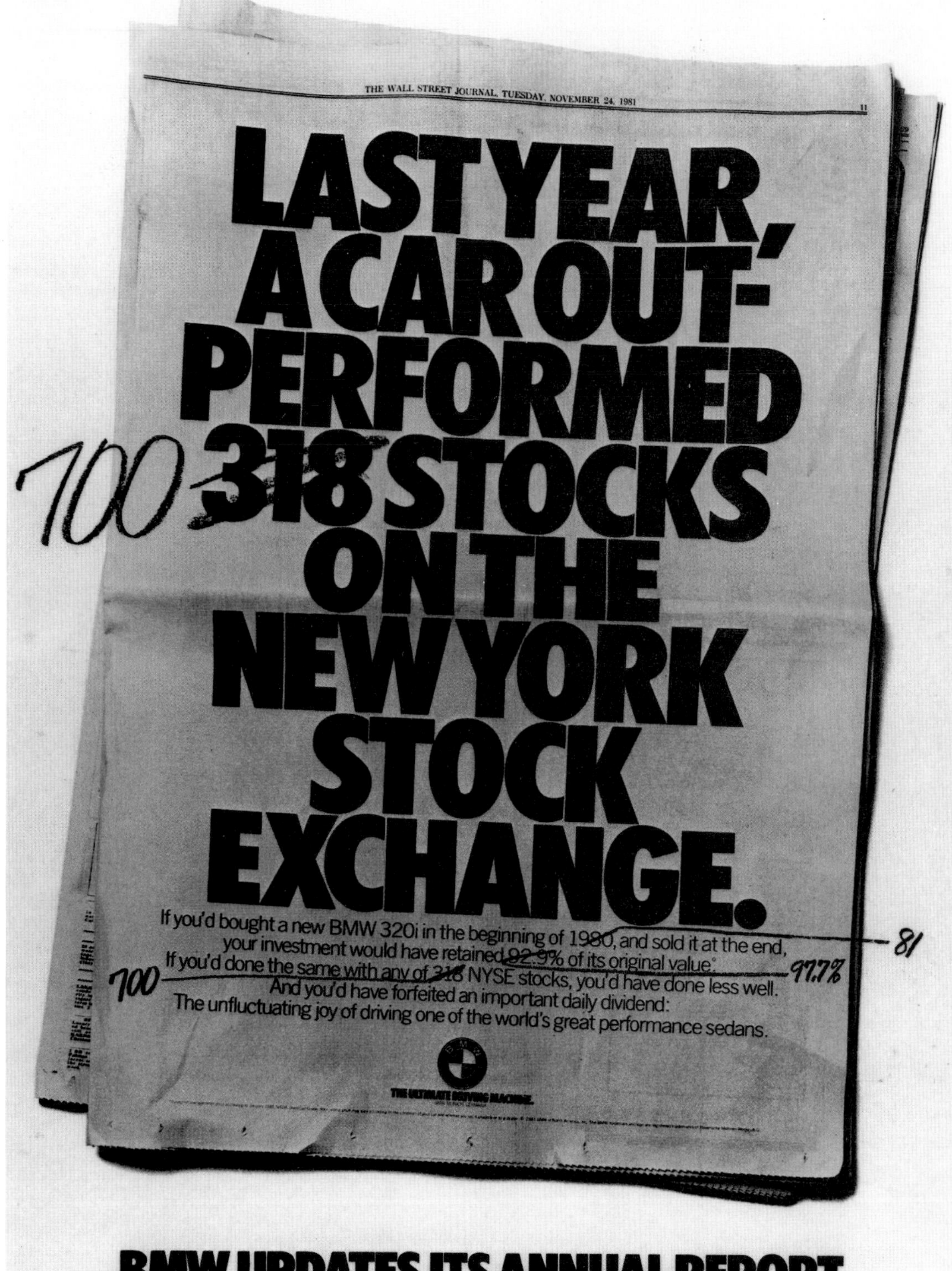

1983

ART DIRECTOR
Anthony Angotti

WRITER
Tom Thomas

DESIGNERS
Anthony Angotti
Barbara Bowman
Dominique Singer

PHOTOGRAPHER
Robert Ammirati

CLIENT
BMW of North America

AGENCY
Ammirati & Puris

The one on the left has claimed more victims.

A nice, comfy floral-patterned armchair? What possible harm could that do to anybody?

According to the latest medical opinion, the answer is plenty.

The people at risk, we're told, are the retired (and nowadays that can mean mere youngsters of 55 or so).

They've worked hard all their lives. Now they feel they deserve to take things a bit easy.

Quite right, too.

The trouble begins when 'taking things easy' turns into lazing in an armchair all day.

Too many naps, too many snoozes, and the body can suddenly decide it's simply not worth waking up again.

The message from the doctors is loud and clear. Don't just sit there. Do something.

Opt for an active retirement, in other words.

You're always daydreaming about the things you wish you'd done with your life.

This will be your chance to do them.

Go ahead, build your ocean-going catamaran. Start up your vegetarian restaurant on Skye. Open that donkey sanctuary in Wales.

There'll be nothing to stop you.

Except money, of course.

And that is why you should be talking to Albany Life.

Not later on in your career. But right now, in your thirties or forties.

Start putting a regular sum into one of our high-growth savings plans and you can build yourself a very nice wodge of capital indeed.

We'll collect every penny of tax relief due to you. We'll then lump the two sums together and invest them on your behalf.

And our investment advice is arguably the best there is.

We retain the services of none other than Warburg Investment Management, a subsidiary of the merchant bank S. G. Warburg & Co. Ltd.

If you'd like to hear more about our retirement savings plans, post off the coupon.

We'd hate to see you sitting in a chair just because you couldn't afford to do anything else.

To learn more about our plans, send this coupon to Peter Kelly, Albany Life Assurance, FREEPOST, Potters Bar EN6 1BR.

Name

Address

Tel:

Name of your Life Assurance Broker, if any:

DT2

Albany Life

A member of the American General Corporation group.

1984

ART DIRECTOR
Andy Lawson

WRITER
Adrian Holmes

PHOTOGRAPHER
Jimmy Wormser

CLIENT
Albany Life Assurance

AGENCY
Lowe Howard-Spink Campbell-Ewald/London

PLEASE BUCKLE UP FOR SECURITY. © 1987 RANGE ROVER OF NORTH AMERICA

We brake for fish.

Would you like to experience a Range Rover under optimum conditions?

Just add water.

A Range Rover can hold its own in water deep enough for a boat.

At the same time, it reaches speeds of roughly 90 knots on the test track. And provides you with the luxury you'd expect in a car priced somewhat above $30,000.

So why not consider a Range Rover?

And convert your money into a liquid asset?

RANGE ROVER

1988

ART DIRECTOR
Roy Grace

WRITER
Diane Rothschild

PHOTOGRAPHER
Carl Furuta

CLIENT
Range Rover of North America

AGENCY
Grace and Rothschild

A man who murdered his parents persuaded psychiatrists to let him live with his aunt and uncle because he loved them "like my own mother and father." Then...

...he murdered them too.

And this is just one true horror story cited by Senator Orrin Hatch in his article, "The Insanity Defense is Insane," written for the October Reader's Digest.

As criminals continue to be acquitted by reason of insanity—and as convicted killers are released from mental hospitals only to kill again—Senator Hatch says we must find a solution to this deadly problem. And he offers one.

It's Digest articles like this that help 40 million readers make sense of an often crazy world.

1983

ART DIRECTOR
Stan Schofield

WRITER
Jim Parry

CLIENT
Reader's Digest

AGENCY
Posey Parry & Quest/
Connecticut

Around Here, High Technology Means Having Your Roasters Up On The Top Floor.

We could probably stretch the facts a little and claim that First Colony has been in the forefront of the high technology revolution. After all, our efforts to bring our customers the finest coffees from around the world include the use of the most up-to-date communication systems. And now we've got a computer hard at work tracking orders all the way from raw product to the retailer's shelf.

But to be perfectly honest, the way we handle the coffee beans themselves just hasn't changed much in four generations.

We still roast our coffees to the right color, not to a fixed amount of time. Our quality control department still consists of an antique cupping table where we've taste tested our coffees since 1902.

And to guarantee freshness, we send our coffees right from the roaster to the loading dock for same-day shipment.

We'd be happy to change our ways if customers ended up with a better product in the process. Bring on the laser roasters and electronic flavor analyzers if they'll make a Kenya AA smoother or a Hawaiian Kona richer.

In the meantime, you can be sure that the First Colony coffees you sell your customers are made using the same methods that made us America's leading specialty coffee company. Every morning, Harvey Groome and his crew will be firing up our trusty old Jabez Burns roasting equipment on the fifth floor.

And until we find better methods or add another floor to our building, that's about as high as most of the technology around here is ever going to get.

The First Colony Coffee & Tea Company

The First Colony Coffee & Tea Company, Inc., Norfolk and San Francisco. Telephone toll-free 800-446-8555.

Our Boss Spends A Lot Of Time Drinking His Troubles Away.

Stop by First Colony any time of the day, or even some evenings, and there's a good chance you'll find our president sitting down with a cup of coffee. Or two cups. Or half a dozen.

Gill Brockenbrough's got a problem that goes back four generations: how to make sure nothing but the finest coffees carry the First Colony name. And he still solves that problem the way his ancestors did. By personally tasting samples of each and every candidate for the First Colony label.

From a practical standpoint, it would probably make sense for the boss to spend a little less time testing coffees at our antique cupping table. The way our business has been growing, there are plenty of other things for him to do. But that's what made us America's leading specialty coffee company in the first place. A commitment to fine coffees that runs generations deep.

Needless to say, the time Gill Brockenbrough spends testing coffees is not all drudgery. The world's best coffees regularly cross our cupping table on their way to our customers. Rare Jamaica Blue Mountain. Rich Sumatra Mandheling. The pick of the East African crop—Tanzania Kilimanjaro and Kenya AA.

But even the most distinguished coffee varieties don't always live up to their names. That's why the president of The First Colony Coffee & Tea Company still insists on drinking his troubles away.

It means you and your customers won't have to.

The First Colony Coffee & Tea Company

The First Colony Coffee & Tea Company, Inc., Norfolk and San Francisco. Telephone toll-free 800-446-8555.

The Day Our Coffees Reach Drinking Age, We Make Them Leave Home.

And around here our coffees are ready to leave home at a tender age indeed.

Because we know the very thing that improves the flavor of fine wines—aging—has exactly the opposite effect on specialty coffees.

So we ship our gourmet coffees the same day they're roasted. We make sure you get the freshest possible product no matter where you live by roasting at both our East and West Coast plants. We're the only roaster to do so.

Of course, getting a rare Celebes Kalossi or a richly flavored Swiss Chocolate Almond to you quickly is meaningless if it isn't of the highest quality in the first place.

At First Colony, we import only select high-grown coffees from the Carribean, Central and South America, Africa, Asia and the Middle East.

Then we roast them to just the right color, to the peak of flavorful perfection. And we still taste test every coffee we sell at the same cupping table our family has used for four generations.

We also work with you on an individual basis to help control your stock, assuring a fresher product and better inventory management.

The First Colony Coffee & Tea Company. Every day we create the finest coffees the world has to offer. Only to leave them homeless.

The First Colony Coffee & Tea Company®

The First Colony Coffee & Tea Company, Inc., Norfolk and San Francisco. Telephone toll-free (800) 446-8555.

1984

ART DIRECTOR
Mark Fuller

WRITERS
Ed Jones
Allen Wimett

PHOTOGRAPHER
Ralph Holland

CLIENT
The First Colony Coffee & Tea Company

AGENCY
Finnegan & Agee/ Richmond, VA

"I may be one of the few people in the world who has seen a canary given an enema."

So says the secretary to the remarkable, diminutive — five-foot-four, 100 pounds — Dr. Gus Eckstein (1890-1981), expert on animal behavior.

In an original article in the June Reader's Digest, Eckstein's secretary recounts her boss's work with birds, mice, cockroaches, etc. — and his magnetic personality that attracted such notables as Sinclair Lewis, Aldous Huxley, Thornton Wilder, Garson Kanin and Helen Hayes (who, walking into Eckstein's lab, had her mink coat attacked by frenzied canaries).

Eckstein "drew people to him by his intensity" — which is how The Digest® draws 39 million readers.

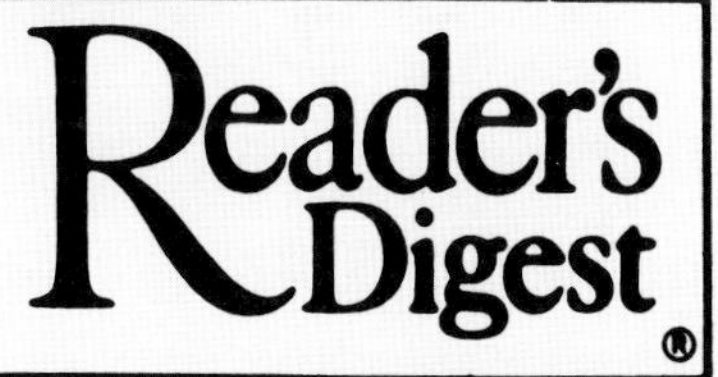

1984
ART DIRECTOR
Vince Ansaldi
WRITER
Jim Parry
CLIENT
Reader's Digest
AGENCY
Posey Parry & Quest/
Connecticut

Ten-year-old Iranian boys are sent onto the battlefield to detonate mines. They are told, "If you return, you'll be executed."

Some of the boys are armed only with plastic keys to heaven because, says Khomeini, if they are killed on the battlefield, they will go directly to heaven. And, they are told, they will be killed regardless.

An original article in the August Reader's Digest reports the grisly facts of the Iran-Iraq war, a war in which 250,000 have already died. How will it end? One Iraqi major answers, "Inshallah" —as God wills it.

The Digest® arms 54 million readers with understanding.

Reader's Digest®

In 1978, a Finnish politician tried to ban Donald Duck. One of the charges against Donald was he hadn't married Daisy Duck.

This attitude, however, is atypical. Today, Donald's films play in 76 countries. And several countries are issuing postage stamps in his honor.

To mark Donald's 50th birthday, an original article in the May Reader's Digest traces the careers of Donald and 79-year-old Clarence Nash, who has *been* Donald from the beginning—ever since he walked into Walt Disney's small studio and rendered "Mary Had a Little Lamb" in Duckspeak.

55 million readers take to The Digest® like ducks to water.

Reader's Digest®

It is known that one way to avoid getting malaria is to sleep with a pig– so mosquitoes bite him instead of you. It is not known what the pig thinks of this arrangement.

A great many mosquitoes (there are some 3000 species and subspecies) would rather dine on some animal other than man. Which, inasmuch as mosquitoes transmit malaria, yellow fever, dengue and encephalitis, you might want to encourage.

The July Reader's Digest sadly reports that swatting a few hundred mosquitoes per day is like "trying to ladle out the ocean with a teaspoon." So "consider giving up and going inside." Perhaps with a pig.

54 million people read The Digest® every month—a very nice arrangement.

1985

ART DIRECTOR
Vince Ansaldi

WRITER
Jim Parry

CLIENT
Reader's Digest

AGENCY
Posey Parry & Quest/Connecticut

Perception.

Reality.

AMERICAN EXPRESS
3712 345678 95006
C F FROST
If you think you can calculate the net worth of a Rolling Stone reader by emptying his right front pocket, you should check what he's carrying around in his right rear pocket. One and a half million Rolling Stone readers are card carrying capitalists. Cash in on the action in Rolling Stone. Source: Simmons 1984
Rolling Stone
©Straight Arrow Publishers, Inc., 1985

1986

ART DIRECTOR
Nancy Rice

WRITER
Bill Miller

PHOTOGRAPHER
Jim Marvy

CLIENT
Rolling Stone

AGENCY
Fallon McElligott/
Minneapolis

Lowest cost per millionaire.

BARRON'S
NATIONAL BUSINESS AND FINANCIAL WEEKLY
Holy Cow! Is This Bull for Real? Page 6
Phelps Dodge:
Out Of The Pits?

Ads like this usually congratulate themselves on their alluring cost-per-thousand figures.

And ours are more alluring than most: Barron's has a lower overall CPM than Business Week, Forbes or Fortune. Period.

But we point you now to a more revealing set of numbers—the sort that show up not on media plans but on personal statements of net worth.

Almost one third (31%) of Barron's readers come from households with a net worth of $1 million or more.* Which is substantially more than the competition.

That works out to a little more than two and a half cents a millionaire. Which is substantially *less* than the competition.

So if you're looking to reach an upscale audience, no one will take you to the top of that scale as effectively as Barron's.

And no one charges as little for the trip.

BARRON'S
HOW THE SMART MONEY GETS THAT WAY.

*Source: *Survey of Adults and Markets of Affluence*, 1985, Mendelsohn Media Research, Inc. CPM's are based on 7" x 10" black and white units for all publications.

1987
ART DIRECTOR
Anthony Angotti
WRITER
Tom Thomas
CLIENT
Barron's Trade
AGENCY
Angotti Thomas Hedge

BOB LAMBERT · RETOUCHING · 835-2166

1987

ART DIRECTOR
Tom Lichtenheld

WRITER
Mike Lescarbeau

ARTIST
Bob Lambert

PHOTOGRAPHER
Stock

CLIENT
Bob Lambert

AGENCY
Fallon McElligott/
Minneapolis

Perception.

Reality.

If you think a plate of homemade brownies can satisfy the munchies of a Rolling Stone reader, here's the scoop on what else it takes. Last week, Rolling Stone readers spent 290 million dollars in grocery stores, drank 40 million glasses of soda, ate 6 million cups of yogurt and polished off 4 million candy bars. And they're still hungry.

Rolling Stone

Perception.

Reality.

(Scratch and sniff.)

(Scratch and sniff.)

If your olfactory impression of Rolling Stone readers smells like something far out or far east, take a whiff of this: Last week alone, Rolling Stone readers used the world's most fashionable fragrances 34 million times. If you've got fragrances to sell, Rolling Stone can hit your target right on the nose.

Rolling Stone

Perception.

Reality.

If you still think Rolling Stone readers are trying to get a grip on what life is all about, check their score on what life after five is all about. Last year, Rolling Stone readers served up $50 million dollars worth of recreational purchases. If you've got sporting goods to sell, you just hit the sweet spot.

Rolling Stone

1987
ART DIRECTOR
Houman Pirdavari
WRITER
Bill Miller
PHOTOGRAPHER
Rick Dublin
CLIENT
Rolling Stone
AGENCY
Fallon McElligott/ Minneapolis

(OPPOSITE) ▶
1980
ART DIRECTOR
Roger Mosconi
WRITER
Penny Hawkey
AGENCY PRODUCERS
Jean-Claude Kaufmann
Karen Scanlon
PRODUCTION COMPANY
N. Lee Lacy
DIRECTOR
N. Lee Lacy
CLIENT
Coca-Cola
AGENCY
McCann-Erickson

(SFX: STADIUM NOISES)

COP: Please, please, you can't go down there.

(SFX: STADIUM NOISES)

BOY: Mr Greene . . . Mr Greene.

GREENE: Yeah.

BOY: You . . . you need any help?

GREENE: Uh, uh!

BOY: I just want you to know . . . I think . . . I think you're the best ever.

GREENE: Yeah . . . sure.

BOY: You . . . you want my Coke?

GREENE: Nah . . .

BOY: It's okay . . . you can have it. Really, you can have it!

GREENE: Okay . . . thanks.

SINGERS: *A Coke and a smile.*
Makes me feel good.
Makes me feel nice.

BOY: See you around

SINGERS: *That's the way it should be. I like to see . . .*

GREENE: Hey, kid!

SINGERS: *. . . the whole world smiling at me.*

GREENE: *Here . . . catch!*

SINGERS: *Coca Cola adds life . . .*

BOY: Wow . . . thanks Mean Joe!

SINGERS: *. . . have a Coke and a smile!*

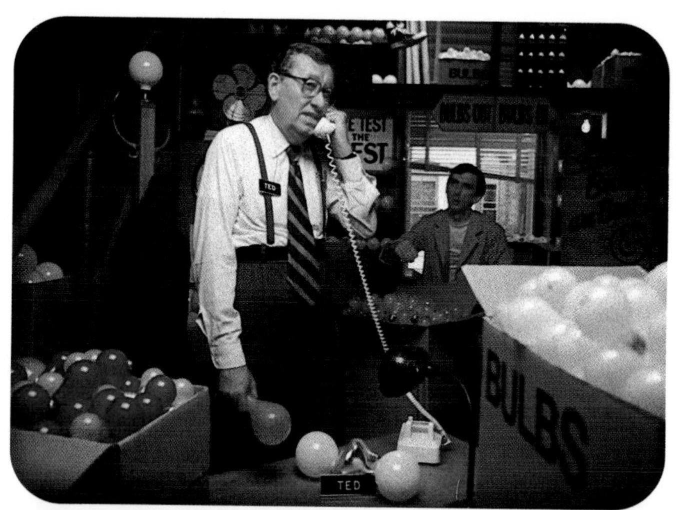

DAYS LATER

GUY VO: Would you please be so kind as to listen? I'm telling you, if I don't have that package on my desk by tomorrow, you understand. If I don't have that package on my desk by tomorrow, and Frank here will bear me out. My dear friend, I am out of business.

(SFX: SCREECH OF TRUCK)

(SILENCE)

ANNCR VO: Next time, send it Federal Express. When it absolutely, positively has to be there overnight.

1980

ART DIRECTOR
Michael Tesch

WRITER
Patrick Kelly

AGENCY PRODUCER
Maureen Kearns

PRODUCTION COMPANY
Sëdëlmaier Films

DIRECTOR
Joe Sëdëlmaier

CLIENT
Federal Express

AGENCY
Ally & Gargano

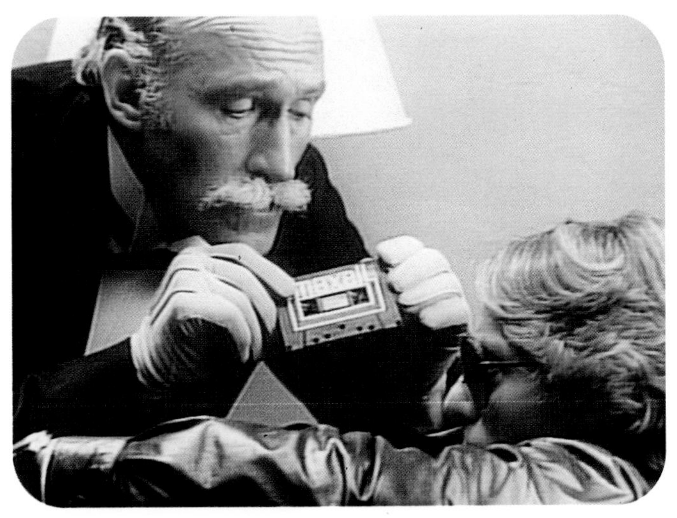

VO: Even after 500 plays . . .
(SFX: MUSIC EXPLODES)
. . . our high fidelity tape still delivers high fidelity.
Maxell. it's worth it.

1981

ART DIRECTOR
Lars Anderson
WRITER
Peter Levathes
AGENCY PRODUCER
Dane Johnson
PRODUCTION COMPANY
Sandbank Films
DIRECTOR
Henry Sandbank
CLIENT
Maxell
AGENCY
Scali McCabe Sloves

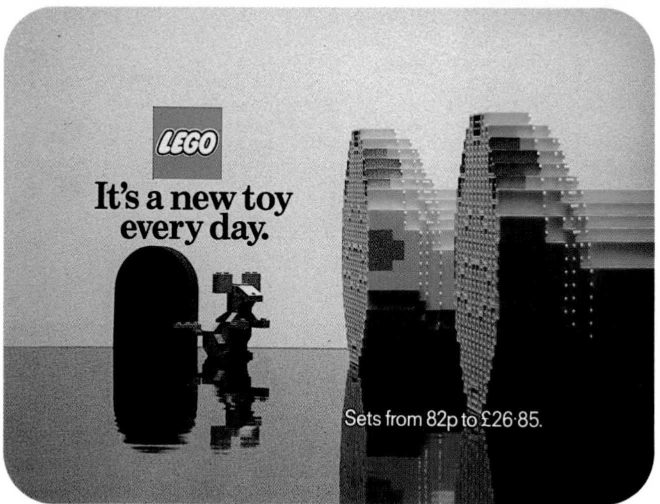

MVO: You see I was standing outside my mousehole the other day . . .
When all of a sudden along comes this cat.
So quick as a flash, I turned into a dog. (Ruff, Ruff)
But the cat turned into a dragon.
So I turned into a fire engine. How's that. (Chuckle)
And then, and then he turned into a submarine.
So I became a submarine-eating kipper. I said a kipper not a slipper.
Thank you very much. (Chuckle)
But he turned into an anti-kipper ballistic missile.
So I turned into a missile cruncher. Crunch, crunch, crunch, crunch, crunch.
Just in time to see him change into a very, very big elephant. So do you know what I did then? . . .
I turned back into a mouse and gave him the fright of his life.

MVO: Lego. It's a new toy every day.

1981

ART DIRECTOR
Graham Watson

WRITER
Mike Cozens

AGENCY PRODUCER
Jane Bearman

PRODUCTION COMPANY
Clearwater Films

DIRECTOR
Ken Turner

CLIENT
Lego (U.K.)

AGENCY
TBWA/London

(SFX: BAR NOISES)

MADDEN: Excuse me. I'm not the same crazy coach who used to storm around the sidelines yelling at the officials. I've learned to relax, and I drink Lite Beer from Miller.
Do you know that Lite's got a third less calories than their regular beer? And listen to this. Lite doesn't fill me up.
Besides that, Lite tastes fantastic. Oh sure, there are a lot of other beers around and you can drink any one you want.
But let me tell you this:
For my money . . .

ANNCR VO: Lite Beer from Miller. Everything you always wanted in a beer. And less.

MADDEN: I say why drink anything else.
As I was saying, I don't care what anybody thinks . . .

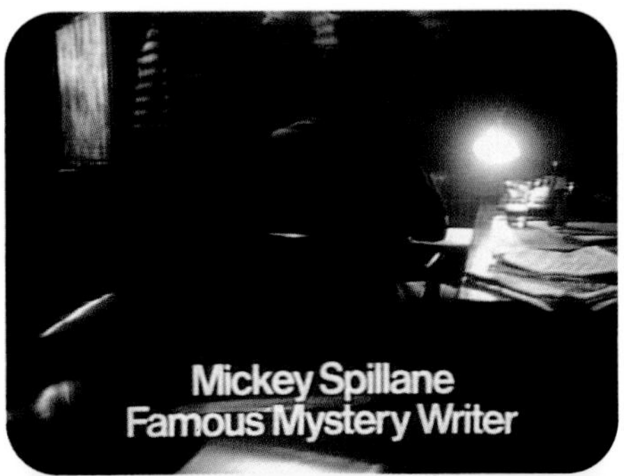

(SFX: TYPING)

MICKEY VO: Chapter 9. I kicked in the door and shouted 'freeze' to the lone figure in the room. Even in the darkness I could see she was the most beautiful woman I ever met.
Suddenly I saw the Lite Beer from Miller.
'It's got a third less calories than their regular beer. And it's less filling,' she whispered. 'But the best thing is it tastes so great.'
Suddenly all the pieces fell into place. And I knew I had come to the end of a long, long road.
She poured, we drank. To be continued.

ANNCR VO: Everything you always wanted in a beer.
And less.

CARLOS: Y'know, one of the best things about coming to America was that I got to try American beers. I tried them all. And the one I like best is Lite Beer from Miller. It's got a third less calories than their regular beer. It's less filling. And it really tastes great. That is why I tell my friends from Mexico, 'When you come to America, drink Lite Beer. But don't drink the water.'

1981

ART DIRECTOR
Nick Gisonde

WRITER
Jeane Bice

AGENCY PRODUCER
Marc Mayhew

PRODUCTION COMPANY
Bob Giraldi Productions

DIRECTOR
Bob Giraldi

CLIENT
Miller Brewing

AGENCY
Backer & Spielvogel

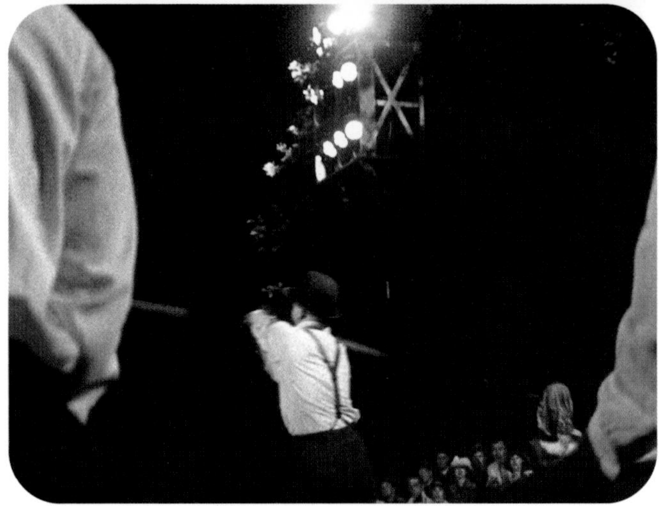

(MUSIC)

ANNCR VO: On a summer's evening in 1924, in Lynn, Massachusetts, perhaps the most significant game in the long history of baseball was played.
It wasn't the pitching that was so extraordinary, nor the hitting. And the fielding, well, it was less than exemplary.
No, what made this game truly historic was the time of day.

(SFX)

Nightfall.
For it was on this night that this small group of GE engineers ushered in the era of night baseball. Baseball under the lights.
And while the names of "Yugo" Fee and Tommy Perkins and Hank Innes will never be recorded in the Hall of Fame . . .
It was this earnest band of GE pioneers that made possible for us all the many brilliant nights to come.

(SFX)

SINGERS: *GE. We bring good things to life.*

1982
ART DIRECTORS
Phil Dusenberry
Ted Sann
WRITERS
Phil Dusenberry
Ted Sann
AGENCY PRODUCER
Jeff Fischgrund
PRODUCTION COMPANY
Bob Giraldi Productions
DIRECTOR
Bob Giraldi
CLIENT
General Electric
AGENCY
BBDO

(OPPOSITE) ▶

1982
ART DIRECTOR
Michael Tesch
WRITER
Patrick Kelly
AGENCY PRODUCER
Maureen Kearns
PRODUCTION COMPANY
Sëdëlmaier Films
DIRECTOR
Joe Sëdëlmaier
CLIENT
Federal Express
AGENCY
Ally & Gargano

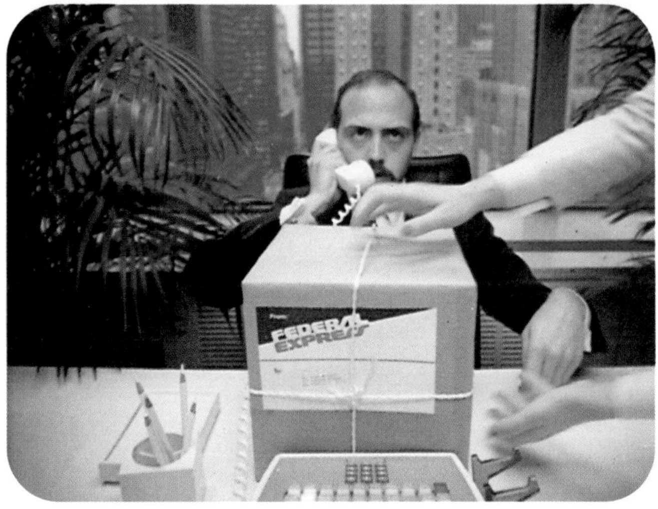

MR SPLEEN VO: OkayEunice,travelplans.IneedtobeinNewYorkon Wednesday,LAonThursday,NewYorkonFriday.Gotit?

EUNICE VO: Got it.

SPLEEN VO: Soyouwanttoworkhere,wellwhatmakesyouthinkyoudeserve ajobhere?

GUY: Wellsir,Ithinkonmyfeet,I'mgoodwithfiguresandIhaveasharpmind.

SPLEEN: Excellent.CanyoustartMonday?

GUY: Yessir.Absolutelywithouthesitation.

SPLEEN: Congratulations,welcomeaboard. (SFX) SPLEEN VO: Wonderful, wonderful,wonderful.AndinconclusionJim,Bill,Paul,Dan,Frank,andTed, businessisbusinessandasweallknow,inordertogetsomethingdone you'vegottodosomething.Inordertodosomethingyou'vegottogetto worksolet'sallgettowork.Thankyouforattendingthismeeting. (SFX) Peteryoudidabangupjobl'mputtingyouinchargeof Pittsburgh.

PETER: Pittsburgh,perfect.

SPLEEN: Iknowit'sperfectPeterthat'swhyIpickedPittsburgh.Pittsburgh's perfectPeter.MayIcallyouPete?

PETER: CallmePete.

SPLEEN: Pete.

SECRETARY VO: There'saMrSnitlerheretoseeyou. SECRETARY: Canyou wait15seconds.

MAN: I'll wait 15 seconds.

SPLEEN VO: CongratulationsonyourdealinDenverDavid.I'mputtingyou downtodealinDallas.Donisitadeal?Dowehaveadeal?It'sadeal.Ihaveacall comingin . . .

ANNCR VO: In this fast moving high pressure, get-it-done-yesterday world . . . Aren't you glad that there's one company that can keep up with it all?

SPLEEN VO: Dickwhat'sthedealwiththedeal.Arewedealing?We'redealing. Daveit'sadealwithDon,DorkandDick.Dorkit'sadealwithDon,Daveand Dick.Dickit'saDorkwithDonDealandDave.Dave,gottago,disconnecting. Dorkgottago,disconnecting.Dickgottago,disconnecting . . .

ANNCR VO: Federal Express. (SFX)
When it absolutely positively has to be there overnight.

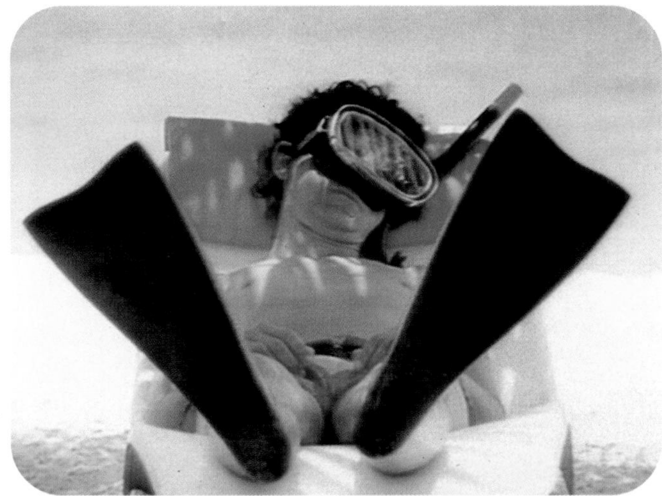

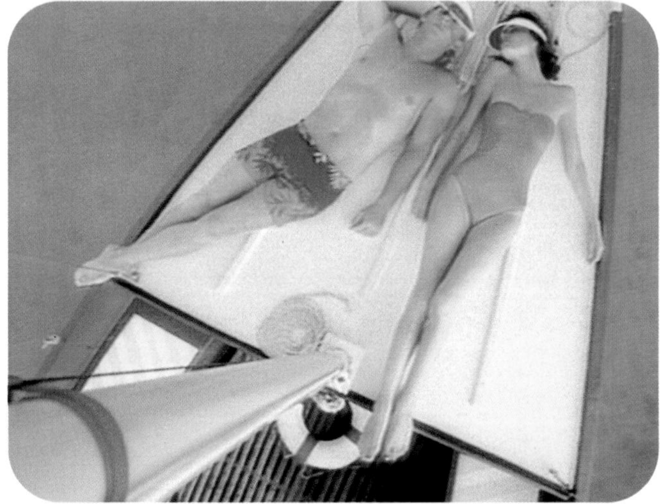

ANNCR: At Club Med you can water ski . . . play tennis . . . snorkel . . . or sail . . . wind surf . . . or play volley ball . . .
At Club Med you can exercise everything. Including your right not to exercise anything.

SONG: *The Club Med vacation. The antidote for civilization.*

1983

ART DIRECTOR
Anthony Angotti

WRITER
Joe O'Neill

AGENCY PRODUCER
Ozzie Spenningsby

PRODUCTION COMPANY
Brooks Fulford
Cramer Seresin

DIRECTOR
Michael Seresin

CLIENT
Club Med

AGENCY
Ammirati & Puris

(MUSIC: UNDER)

MAN: Have you been talking to our son on long distance again?

WOMAN: NODS AND WHIMPERS

MAN: Did he tell you how much he loves you?

WOMAN: NODS AND WHIMPERS

MAN: Did he tell you how well he's doing in school?

WOMAN: NODS AND WHIMPERS AND CRIES

MAN: All those things are wonderful. What on earth are you crying for?

WOMAN: Did you see our long distance bill?

(MUSIC)

ANNCR VO: If your long distance bills are too much, call MCI.
Sure, reach out and touch someone.
Just do it for a whole lot less.

1983

ART DIRECTOR
George Euringer

WRITER
Tom Messner

AGENCY PRODUCER
Jerry Haynes

PRODUCTION COMPANY
Bob Giraldi Productions

DIRECTOR
Bob Giraldi

CLIENT
MCI

AGENCY
Ally & Gargano

GUY: I need that package of slides for a major presentation tomorrow at 10:30 AM.

COMPETITOR: You got it!

GUY: Not noon, not 3:00, 10:30 AM.

COMPETITOR: You got it!

GUY: Listen to me. No slides, no presentation.

COMPETITOR: You got it!

GUY: Well, where is it?

COMPETITOR: You'll get it!

(SFX: BARKING)

ANNCR VO: Next time send it Federal Express. Now Federal schedules delivery by 10:30 AM. So when we say you got it, you'll get it.

1983

ART DIRECTOR
Michael Tesch

WRITER
Patrick Kelly

AGENCY PRODUCER
Maureen Kearns

PRODUCTION COMPANY
Kelly Pictures

DIRECTOR
Patrick Kelly

CLIENT
Federal Express

AGENCY
Ally & Gargano

(OPPOSITE) ▶

1984

ART DIRECTOR
Bob Steigelman

WRITER
Charlie Breen

AGENCY PRODUCERS
Eric Steinhauser
Sally Smith

PRODUCTION COMPANY
Dennis Guy & Hirsch

DIRECTOR
Don Guy

CLIENT
Miller Brewing/High Life

AGENCY
Backer & Spielvogel

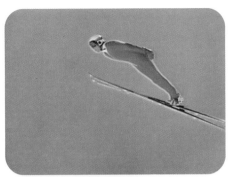

(MUSIC: UNDER)

(SFX: CAR, ALLEY CAT)

ANNCR VO: That kid's out there again. But he's not alone. He's got a dream with him and every night after work he chases that dream, the one that says someday you're going to watch him run 400 meters faster than any other man in the summer games.

(MUSIC: UP)

In the past it probably would have been just a dream but we have an Olympic training center now in Colorado Springs
And he can go there and learn how to run faster than he's ever run before.
So maybe he'll become as good as he believes he can be.
And maybe one summer day when you're watching the '84 games you just might say . . . that kid's out there again.

(CHANT: USA . . . USA)

This American Dream was brought to you by Miller High Life . . .
Sponsor of the U.S. Olympic Training Center.

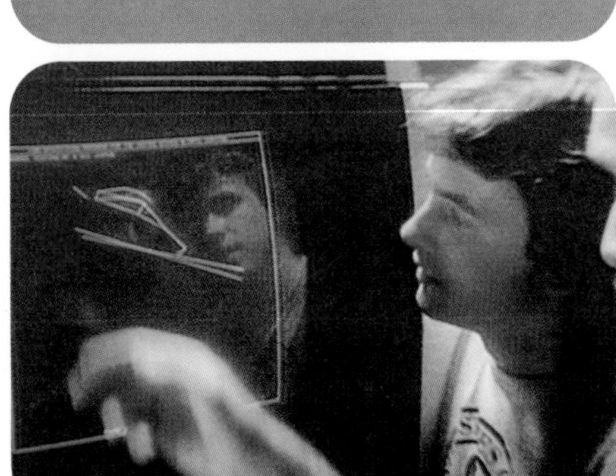

ANNCR VO: They say it's not an American sport but they forgot to tell him.
Because he's got a dream that says one day the world's going to watch him jump farther than any other man in the winter games.
In the past it probably would have been just a dream . . .
But we have an Olympic Training Center now in Colorado Springs and he can go there and find out what he's doing right, what he's doing wrong, and how to fly off a mountainside farther than he's ever flown before.
So maybe it's not just a dream.
And maybe, on a winter day in 1984 . . .

(CHANT UNDER: USA, USA, USA)

They'll stop saying, "It's not an American Sport."
This American dream was brought to you by Miller High Life . . .
The sponsor of the U.S. Olympic Training Center.

(SFX: STREET NOISES)

1ST GUY: Hey, hey here he comes, Tiny . . .

2ND GUY: Yes, here he is ladies and gentlemen, the up and coming . . .

ANNCR: One inch farther, that's how far he wants to throw it today.
And tomorrow an inch farther than that.
Because he's got a dream that says some day he's gonna throw that 16-pound piece of iron farther . . .

SHOT PUTTER VO: Ugh.

ANNCR: . . . than any other man in the summer games.

1ST GUY: You're not gonna win any gold medals doin' that, man.

2ND GUY: Shh, Shh.

(MUSIC: UP)

ANNCR: In the past it probably would have been just a dream but today he just might become as good as he believes he can be . . .

SHOT PUTTER VO: Ugh.

ANNCR: Because today he can go to the U.S. Olympic Training Center in Colorado Springs.
And maybe on a summer day in 1984 . . .
He'll go up against the best in the world and he'll throw it . . . one inch farther.

(CHANT UNDER: USA, USA, USA)

This American Dream was brought to you by Miller High Life . . .
The sponsor of the U.S. Olympic Training Center.

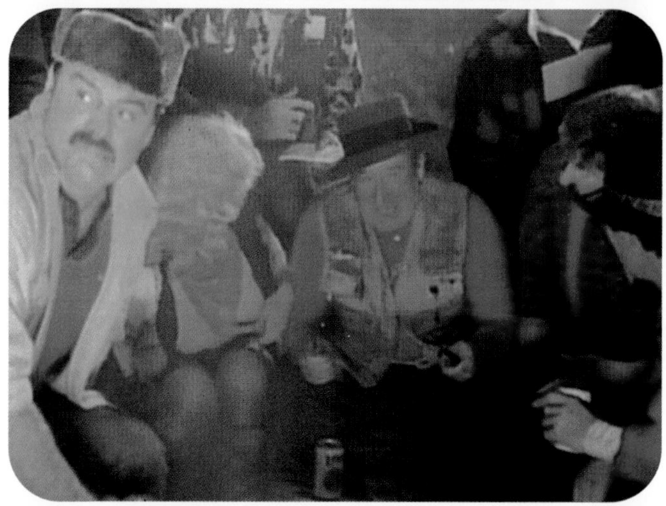

MARV: This camping trip was a good idea.

GRITS: Yeah, it sure is relaxing.

BILLY: Peaceful.

CORKY: Groovy.

GUYS: Groovy.

MADDEN: Kind of dark though.

BUBBA: Man, I'm getting thirsty.

DICK: Yeah, let's have another Light Beer from Miller.

RED: Yeah, Lite's less filling.

TASTE GREAT GROUP: Tastes great.

LESS FILLING GROUP: Less filling!

T.G.: Taste great!

L.F.: Less filling. (SFX: HOWLING)

TOMMY: What was that?

MICKEY SPILLANE: The creature.

DICK W.: What creature?

MICKEY: Well, legend has it that a horrible thing stalks these woods.

LEE: Oooh, Mickey.

RAY: What does this creature look like?

MICKEY VO: It walks on two legs, but it isn't human. It's got big eyes that bulge out and . . . (SFX: FOOTSTEPS)

DICK: It's the creature.

RODNEY: Hey guys, hey guys, where're you going? Hey guys, where are the marshmallows?

ANNCR VO: Lite Beer from Miller. Everything you always wanted in a beer and less.

JOHN: Come on, it's after us.

BUBBA: Man, did you see that thing?

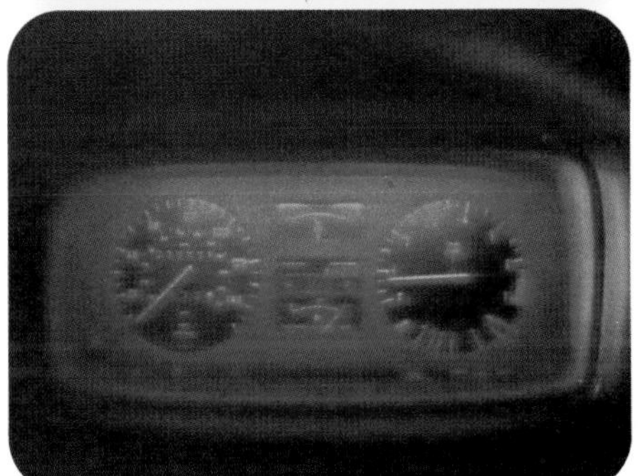

ANNCR VO: Every day, BMW presents a comprehensive report . . . on the state of automotive technology.
Not through some dry dissertation . . . or the theoretical vacuum of a laboratory . . . but rather through a more appropriate vehicle.
The BMW 733i. The luxury sedan that translates the intricacies of technology . . . into that very elusive commodity . . .
. . . called fun.
BMW

ANNCR VO: In Germany . . .
The head of BMW's personnel department is an engineer.
The Head of Corporate Planning . . .
is an engineer.
Even the Chairman . . . is an engineer.
So it's not surprising that BMWs leave the factory with a very clear sense of priorities.
And that's crucial.
Because when you buy a car, what you're buying . . .
Is the company that built it.
BMW

ANNCR VO: For all those confrontations with the unpredictable . . .
. . . BMW introduces the ultimate defense.
The 535i.
With an amazingly agile suspension.
A computer-controlled engine that constantly adjusts to changing driving conditions.
And an ingenious anti-lock braking system.
The BMW 535i.
It lets those who take driving seriously peacefully coexist . . .
. . . with those who don't.
BMW

◀ *(OPPOSITE)*

1985

ART DIRECTOR
Nick Gisonde
WRITER
Charlie Breen
AGENCY PRODUCER
Marc Mayhew
PRODUCTION COMPANY
Bob Giraldi Productions
DIRECTOR
Bob Giraldi
CLIENT
Miller Brewing/Lite Beer
AGENCY
Backer & Spielvogel

1985

ART DIRECTOR
Anthony Angotti
WRITER
Tom Thomas
AGENCY PRODUCERS
Ozzie Spenningsby
Susan Shipman
PRODUCTION COMPANIES
Brooks Fulford
Cramer Seresin
Sandbank Films
DIRECTORS
Michael Seresin
Henry Sandbank
CLIENT
BMW of North America
AGENCY
Ammirati & Puris

Margaret and Tom Fitzgerald

Married, no children
Ages.......30, 31

LAWYER: There's a lot of paperwork here. There's always paperwork when you buy a house. First one says that you lose the house if you don't make your payments. You probobly don't want to think about that but . . . you do have to sign it.
Next says the property is insured for the amount of the note. And you sign that in the lower left corner.
This pretty much says that nobody's got a gun to your head . . . that you're entering this agreement freely.
Next is the house is free of termites. Last one says that the house will be your primary residence and that you won't be relying on rental income to make the payments.
I hope you brought your checkbook. This is the fun part. I say that all the time though most people don't think so. (CHUCKLE)

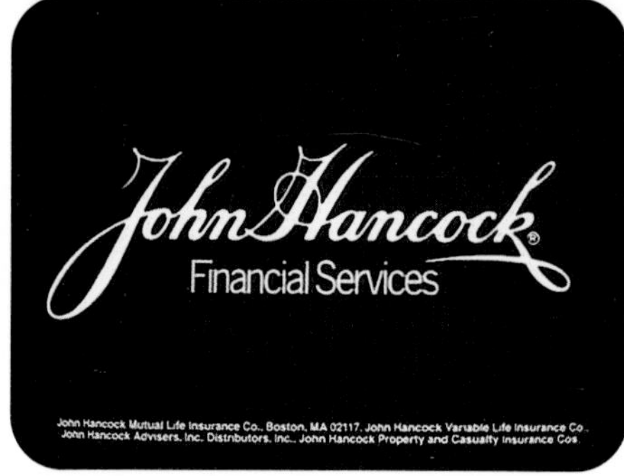

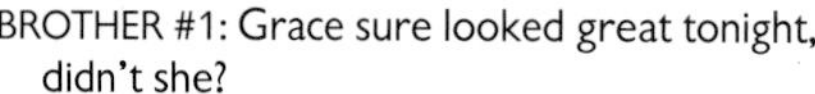

John Hancock Mutual Life Insurance Co., Boston, MA 02117. John Hancock Variable Life Insurance Co.
John Hancock Advisers, Inc. Distributors, Inc., John Hancock Property and Casualty Insurance Cos.

BROTHER #1: Grace sure looked great tonight, didn't she?

BROTHER #2: Yeah.

BROTHER #1: So how you makin' now, huh?

BROTHER #2: I'm going fine . . .

BROTHER #1: You gotta be makin' at least 25.

BROTHER #2: I'm fine . . . maybe a little better than that.

BROTHER #1: 30? Tell me, yes or no, are you making 30?

BROTHER #2: Yes.

BROTHER #1: 30?!

BROTHER #2: Around 30.

BROTHER #1: You got any investments? Any stuff?

BROTHER #2: Got the car.

BROTHER #1: That's not an investment . . . You got an IRA? . . . Life insurance?

BROTHER #2: (SIGH) Not really.

BROTHER #1: You're making 30 and you don't have anything like that? What do you think? You're 18 years old or something?

Real life, real answers.

(SFX: CLAPPING)

(SFX: CLAPPING)

MAN: I've never felt older in my life. (SIGH)
Yesterday, I was a football player. Today, I'm retired.
How do I want to be remembered?
As a good father.
As a good husband.
And that's it.
That's life.
And that's what life is.

1986

ART DIRECTOR
Don Easdon

WRITER
Bill Heater

AGENCY PRODUCER
Mary Ellen Argentieri

PRODUCTION COMPANY
Pytka

DIRECTOR
Joe Pytka

CLIENT
John Hancock

AGENCY
Hill Holliday Connors Cosmopulos/Boston

FRANK: Well, the new Bartles and Jaymes premium wine cooler is finally in the bottle, and our marketing director, Gary Cox, is now getting ready to put it into distribution in major markets. Please buy some, because frankly from our point of view there's no other wine cooler anywhere that's nearly as good at any price. It would also be a personal favor to Ed, because he took out that second on his house and pretty soon he's got a big balloon payment coming up. Thank you and we hope you enjoy our new premium wine cooler.

1986

ART DIRECTOR
Gerald Andelin

WRITER
Hal Riney

AGENCY PRODUCER
Deborah Martin

PRODUCTION COMPANY
Pytka

DIRECTOR
Joe Pytka

CLIENT
E&J Gallo Winery

AGENCY
Hal Riney & Partners/
San Francisco

(SFX: ELECTRICAL BUZZING; MUSIC)

SMITH: Okay, Jonathan . . .

SMITH: We're ready to send you back in time.

DOC: Now remember, you're going back before television, before radio, even before soft drinks.

SMITH: But you're only there to observe. Don't say a word.

DOC: The slightest thing you do or say could change the entire course of history.

JONATHAN: Don't worry, Doc. Mum's the word.

DOC: Okay. Activate time travel mode retrograde to the year 1885.

(SFX: MECHANICAL WHIRRING NOISE)

SMITH: He's there.

DOC: We did it! Hey, where's my Pepsi?

SMITH: It's, oh, no. He took it. This could be catastrophic. It could change history.

DOC: Relax, Smith. You don't really think that one can of Pepsi could alter 100 years of history, do you?

(SFX: VANISHING SOUND)

SMITH: Nah, I guess not.

(SFX: VANISHING SOUND)

DOC: After all, what could 12 little ounces of Pepsi do?

(SFX: VANISHING SOUND)

SMITH: Yeah, you're probably right. What could happen?

DOC: What could happen?

VO: Pepsi. The choice of a new generation.

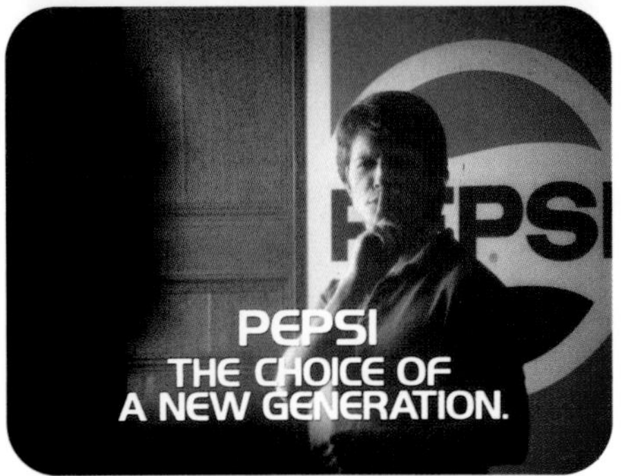

(SFX: FOOTSTEPS CROSSING LIBRARY FLOOR)

(SFX: M.J. FOX DROPS BOOK ON TABLE)

M.J.FOX: Hmmmm.

(SFX: BOOK DROPS LOUDLY ON COPIER MACHINE)

M.J. FOX: Somebody have any . . .

STUDENT: Sssh!

M.J. FOX: Change?

(SFX: SNAPS FINGERS; CLAPS HANDS; COPIER MACHINE MAKES PHOTOCOPY OF PEPSI CAN)

(SFX: PICK UP PHOTOCOPY)

(SFX: SQUEAK OF MOISTURE ON CAN; SOUND OF PHOTOCOPY BEING ROLLED INTO A CAN)

(SFX: CAN OPENING SOUND)

(SFX: FIZZING SOUND)

M.J.FOX: WHISTLES

(SFX: DRINKING SOUNDS)

M.J.FOX: Ahhh.

STUDENT: Ssssh!

(SFX: CAN CRUSHING; CAN BANGING IN METAL GARBAGE CAN)

M.J.FOX: Ssssh!

VO: Pepsi. The choice of a new generation.

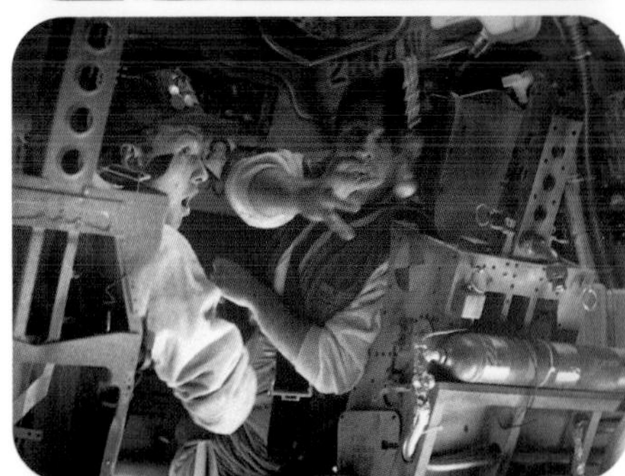
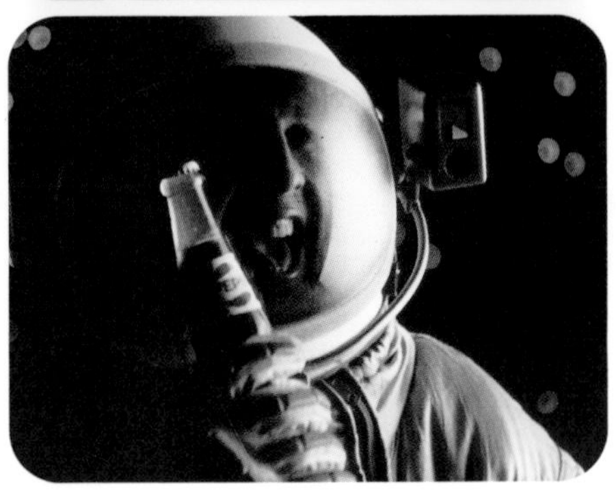

COMMAND CONTROL: Good work, Starship. We'll talk to you at O-six-hundred.

PILOT #1: That's a copy.

COMMAND CONTROL: Why don't you guys take a break?

PILOT #2: How 'bout a Pepsi?

(SFX: BUTTON PRESSED; LATCH OPENS)

PILOT #1: There's only one left.

(SFX: WALTZ MUSIC)

(SFX: HATCH OPENING)

VO: Pepsi. The choice of a new generation.

1987

ART DIRECTORS
Len McCarron
Bruce Dundore
Harvey Hoffenberg

WRITERS
Ted Sann
Rick Meyer
Barry Udoff

AGENCY PRODUCERS
David Frankel
Gene Lofaro
Jerry Cammisa

PRODUCTION COMPANIES
Jennie & Company
Pytka

DIRECTORS
Terry Bedford
Joe Pytka

CLIENT
Pepsi-Cola

AGENCY
BBDO

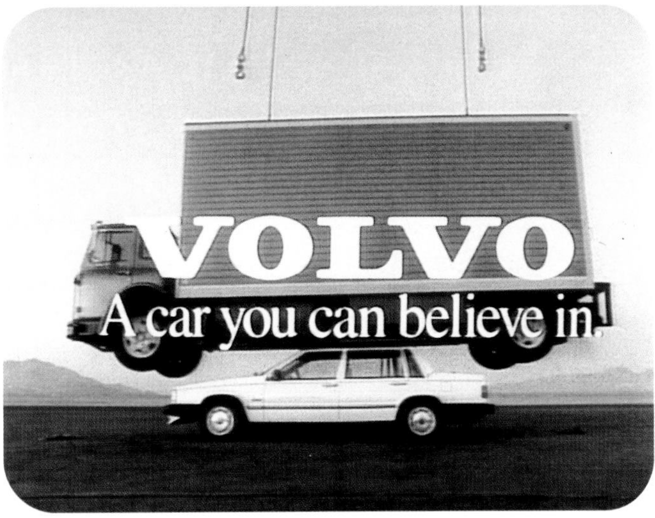
VOLVO
A car you can believe in.

(MUSIC: THROUGHOUT)

(SFX: CLICK)

ANNCR VO: How well does your car stand up to heavy traffic?

(MUSIC: OUT)

1988

ART DIRECTOR
Earl Cavanah

WRITER
Larry Cadman

AGENCY PRODUCER
Jaki Keuch

PRODUCTION COMPANY
Sandbank Films

DIRECTOR
Henry Sandbank

CLIENT
Volvo

AGENCY
Scali McCabe Sloves

ANNCR VO: Maybe it's because meteors fell from the sky that night.
Or because a day is only 24 hours long.
Or could it be because air turned out lighter than water?
All we know is, whatever had to happen happened just right.
In a town called Vergeze. At a spring called Perrier.
It's perfect. It's Perrier.

1988
ART DIRECTOR
Gerald Andelin
WRITERS
Dan Mountain
Peter Murphy
Sally Gill
AGENCY PRODUCER
Sue Rugtiv
PRODUCTION COMPANY
Pytka
DIRECTOR
Joe Pytka
CLIENT
Perrier Group
AGENCY
Hal Riney & Partners/
San Francisco

(OPPOSITE) ▶

1988
ART DIRECTORS
Logan Wilmont
Nick Scott
WRITERS
Mike Court
Richard Spencer
AGENCY PRODUCER
Debbie Court
PRODUCTION COMPANY
Sid Roberson
DIRECTOR
Simon Delaney
CLIENT
Mates Healthcare
AGENCY
Still Price Court Twivy
D'Souza/London

MAN: I'll get it.
(SUBTITLE: THIS'LL IMPRESS HER)

GIRL: No, you always pay.
(SUBTITLE: HE ISN'T MADE OF MONEY)

MAN: I insist.
(SUBTITLE: OR DO I?)

MAN: Are you sure?
(SUBTITLE: PHEW!)

GIRL: It's eight each.
(SUBTITLE: AND WORTH EVERY PENNY)

MAN: Oooooops!
(SUBTITLE: AAAAARRRRRRGGGGHHHHHH!)
(SUBTITLE: !#*!)

GIRL: I think you've dropped something.
(SUBTITLE: BET HE FEELS AN IDIOT)

MAN: Er, I don't know what to say.
(SUBTITLE: WHAT AN IDIOT)

GIRL: Don't say anything.
(SUBTITLE: I THINK YOU'RE VERY SENSIBLE)

GIRL: Shall we go?

VO: Mates are a new range of condoms. Like other condoms, they're reliable. But they're cheaper. It doesn't matter who carries them as long as one of you does.

MAN: Thanks for a lovely evening.
(SUBTITLE: SHAME I RUINED IT)

GIRL: Thank you.
(SUBTITLE: SHAME IT'S OVER)

MAN: See you again next week?
(SUBTITLE: HARDLY WORTH ASKING)

GIRL: Of course:
(SUBTITLE: I THOUGHT HE'D NEVER ASK)

VO: Mates. You make love. They make sense.

(SFX: HALF-SECOND SILENCE; SHOP DOORBELL)

ASSISTANT: Hello.

BOY: Yes . . . er . . . I'd er . . . well . . .
(SUBTITLE: OH, NO! IT'S A WOMAN)

ASSISTANT: Yes?
(SUBTITLE: HE WANTS SOME CONDOMS)

BOY: I want some co..cotton wool.
(SUBTITLE: I REALLY WANT SOME CONDOMS)

ASSISTANT: Of course, will there be anything else?
(SUBTITLE: SILLY QUESTION)

(SFX: CASH REGISTER RING)

BOY: Yeah. Have you got a packet of . . . tissues?
(SUBTITLE: JUST ASK HER)

ASSISTANT: Man-size tissues. Is that all?
(SUBTITLE: JUST ASK ME)

(SFX: CASH REGISTER RING)

VO: Mates are a new range of condoms. Like other condoms, they're reliable. But they're cheaper. She sells hundreds of packets. She's not embarrassed. So why should you be?

BOY: And a packet of Mates Condoms, please.

ASSISTANT: Of course.
(SUBTITLE: AT LAST)
(SUBTITLE: NO SWEAT)

ASSISTANT (TO BACK ROOM): Mr Williams, how much are these Mates Condoms?

VO: Mates. You make love. They make sense.

(SFX: MUSIC TO "ONE MORE NIGHT")

GIRL: Great album, this, isn't it?
(SUBTITLE: YOU'RE GORGEOUS)

BOY: Yeah, great album.
(SUBTITLE: I WANT TO KISS YOUR NECK)

GIRL: What time is your last train?
(SUBTITLE: HOPE YOU MISSED IT)

BOY: Oh no, I've missed it.
(SUBTITLE: NOT FOR 45 MINUTES)

GIRL: Well, you could always stay here.
(SUBTITLE: WILL HE THINK I'M EASY?)

BOY: Well, if it's no trouble. I could stay on the couch.
(SUBTITLES: BE COOL!; DON'T BE PUSHY)

GIRL: Well, you could.
(SUBTITLE: DON'T BE SILLY)

BOY: Grand enough.
(SUBTITLE: WILL SHE BE UPSET IF WE USE A CONDOM?)

GIRL: Well, that's settled then.
(SUBTITLE: WILL HE BE UPSET IF WE USE A CONDOM?)

VO: Mates are a new range of condoms. Like other condoms, they're reliable but they're cheaper. They'll help prevent pregnancy and sexually transmitted diseases. But only if you're not embarrassed about using them.

BOY: I've been waiting for this moment for ages.
(SUBTITLE: WE WILL USE A CONDOM)

GIRL: Funny, I was just thinking the same thing.

VO: Mates. You make love, they make sense.

VO: First came the Danes. Then the Vikings. The Normans. The Saxons. All of them found Ireland absolutely irresistible. So think what a grand time we'd show you Yanks. Especially since you'd be the only ones of the lot we actually invited.

SUPER: IRELAND.
THE ANCIENT BIRTHPLACE OF GOOD TIMES.

1989

ART DIRECTOR
Cathie Campbell

WRITERS
Joe O'Neill
Richard Pels

AGENCY PRODUCER
Pam Ferman

PRODUCTION COMPANY
Berkofsky Smillie
Barrett Productions

DIRECTOR
Peter Smillie

CLIENT
Irish Tourist Board

AGENCY
Hill Holliday

MAN: I'd produce a Broadway show starring me.

ANNCR: New York Lotto. All you need is a dollar and a dream.

WOMAN: I'd go straight to Paris and all I'd pack is a toothbrush and my wallet.

ANNCR: New York Lotto. All you need is a dollar and a dream.

PAMELA: I'd buy out my company and have my boss work for me.

ANNCR: New York Lotto. All you need is a dollar and a dream.

1989

ART DIRECTOR
Ray Groff

WRITER
Nicole Cranberg

AGENCY PRODUCER
Barbara Benedict

PRODUCTION COMPANY
BFCS

DIRECTOR
Bob Brooks

CLIENT
New York State Lottery

AGENCY
DDB Needham Worldwide

(MUSIC: UP)

GIBSON: Bo knows baseball.

EVERETT: Bo knows football.

JORDAN: Bo knows basketball, too.

McENROE: Bo knows tennis?

BENOIT: Bo knows running.

(MUSIC: STOP)

GRETZKY: No.

(MUSIC: UP)

WOMEN: Bo knows cycling.

WEIGHTLIFTERS: Bo knows weights.

(OUT-OF-TUNE MUSIC)

DIDDLEY: Bo . . . you don't know diddley!

(MUSIC: UP)

1989

ART DIRECTOR
Michael Prieve

WRITER
Jim Riswald

AGENCY PRODUCER
Bill Davenport

PRODUCTION COMPANY
Pytka

DIRECTOR
Joe Pytka

CLIENT
Nike

AGENCY
Wieden & Kennedy/
Portland, OR

(SFX: INTERCOM-LIKE BUZZ)

PICKING: Sara. Is the WATS line free?

SARA: No, Mr Picking, it isn't.

PICKING: Call me when it is.

SARA: Sure will. (BUZZ) Yes?

LORD: Sara. I'd like the WATS line?

SARA: Sorry, Mr Lord. Mr Picking's next in line.

LORD: Forget Picking. Put me next.

SARA: Sure will. (BUZZ) Yes?

PICKING: Picking here. Is the WATS free yet?

SARA: Listen, Mr Picking. Mr Lord says his call should be next.

PICKING: We'll see about that. (BUZZ)

SARA: Yes?

KELLY: It's Mr Kelly. Give me the WATS line.

SARA: Mr Picking and Mr Lord are waiting too, Mr Kelly.

KELLY: Whose name is on your check every week, Sara?

SARA: Why, I believe the line is free now.

ANNCR: If you spend more in time than you save in money with Bell's WATS line, call MCI. The nation's long distance phone company. MCI offers your company many economical alternatives to Bell's services. Including one that will save you 30 percent more than their famous WATS line. So call MCI. Because your company hasn't been calling too much. You've just been paying too much.

(SFX: A PHONE RINGS. THEN A VERY TIRED WOMAN'S VOICE)

MOM: Hullo?

DAVE: Hi, Mom. Surprise. It's Dave.

MOM: Hullo?

DAVE: Mom. Wake up. It's your son, Dave. I'm calling long distance.

MOM (STILL ASLEEP BUT KNOWS HIS NAME): Dave?

DAVE: I'm sorry I'm calling so late, but the rates are cheapest weekdays after 11 PM.

MOM: SOUND OF FEMALE SNORING

DAVE: Mom? Mom! Come on. Give the phone to Dad . . .

MOM: Here, Frank. It's for you.

DAD: LOUD MASCULINE SNORING

DAVE: Dad. It's me. Dave. Dad? Come on, Dad. Mom. Are you still there? (SOUND OF TWO PEOPLE SNORING) Wake Dad! Wake Dad! Don't do this to me. Mom . . . Dad . . .

ANNCR: Reach out. Reach out and wake someone. That's one suggestion on how to get Bell's lowest rates on long distance calls. Want a better suggestion? Try MCI, the nation's long distance phone company, and save 30, 40, even 50 percent weekdays by calling after the very decent hour of 5 PM . . . So call MCI. And find out how to save money when you want to. Not when Bell tells you to.

(SFX: PHONE RINGS; FUMBLING WITH RECEIVER IS HEARD; A VERY SLEEPY VOICE SAYS . . .)

DENISE: Hullo?

HAROLD: Denise? It's me. Harold. Did I wake you?

DENISE: Not yet. But if you keep talking, you will.

HAROLD: Come on. This is a long distance call.

DENISE: What time is it?

HAROLD: 2 AM your time.

DENISE: Harold. I have to wake up all over again in four hours. Call me in the morning.

HAROLD: Denise. Wait. I can't. Look how much money I save by calling weekdays after 11 PM.

DENISE: I can save you even more money, Harold.

HAROLD: How?

(SFX: RECEIVER BEING HUNG UP)

ANNCR: Bell suggests that to save the most money on your long distance calls, you should call after 11 PM. We have a better suggestion: call MCI, the nation's long distance phone company, and save 30, 40 even 50 percent between the civilized weekday hours of 5 and 11 PM. Not to mention the savings you can get all day long and weekends. So call MCI now. And stop talking in someone else's sleep.

1982
WRITER
Helayne Spivak
AGENCY PRODUCER
Jerry Haynes
CLIENT
MCI
AGENCY
Ally & Gargano

JOHN CLEESE: Hallo there. Look, apparently last time I was on the radio, talking about this frightfully good rather sophisticated English candy, when I said the name of the people who make this candy, which is Callard and Bowser, I didn't say Callard and Bowser terribly clearly and so all you good American persons have been going into Supermarkets and Drugstores asking for Bollard and Trouser, and Callous and Grocer, Gizzard and Powder, so let's get the name straight, shall we, it's Callard and Bowser. Callard . . . Cal as in *Cal*vin Coolidge and lard as Jess Wil*lard* and Bowser, that's Bow as in the *Bau*haus, or better still Mutiny on the *Boun*ty and ser, as in Panzer Division. So if you want to try the best most sophisticated and upper class candy we make in England, it's quite simple, all you have to do is think of *Cal*vin Coolidge and Jess Wil*lard*, and as in Hans Christian *An*dersen and then the *Bau*haus or Mutiny on the *Boun*ty and a panzer Division, Callard and Bowser. It may take a little time to get hold of but I think you'll find it's worth it.

JOHN CLEESE: Hallo, have you heard about this rather unusual English candy which has a more sophisticated kind of taste than regular candy, not quite as sweet but a very fine classy sort of taste, and it's made by an English firm called Callard and Bowser and it really is jolly good. In fact, the truth is, it's jolly, jolly good, and you'll like it, and as I say it is English so please buy it because we need the money in England at the moment, I mean we're all as poor as church mice now, servants are unbelievably expensive and our industry's practically disappeared, about all we make is muffins and cricket bats and really good candy and half the cricket bats come from Hong Kong, so please, do us a favour and just try this Callard and Bowser candy, its rather sophisticated taste and I'm sure you'll approve of it and after all, I mean we did fight on your side in the War and we always let you beat us at golf and incidentally, let's not forget you pinched our language, if we hadn't forgotten to copyright that you'd be paying us the most amazing royalties every week so instead please buy Callard and Bowser's rather sophisticated English candy and help England back on its feet, frankly I think it's the least you could do.

JOHN CLEESE: Hallo . . . Um . . . look there's some frightfully good rather sophisticated English candy now being sold in the US of A, it's terribly popular among the upper classes here in England so please do try some. It's called Callard and Bowser candy and it's butterscotch and toffee and toffee comes in seven exciting new flavours, Raspberry, Aubergine, Smoky Passionfruit, Mackerel, Pork and Prune, Lamb and Banana, and the flavour of the month Leather, Tangerine and Raccoon, a new taste sensation . . . I'm sorry those aren't the flavours at all, I made them up, it was a cheap trick to catch your attention, and I'm very ashamed of myself because the real flavours are perfectly sensible and quite delicious, and rather sophisticated because Callard and Bowser candy isn't quite as sweet as ordinary candy, so it appeals to rather sophisticated urbane, educated people who wouldn't like silly publicity stunts about Leather Tangerine and Raccoon-flavoured toffee at all. So please forgive me; completely ignore this commercial. Forget all about it and simply try some of Callard and Bowser's candy and I promise not to be naughty again.

1983
WRITERS
John Cleese
Lynn Stiles
AGENCY PRODUCER
Robert L. Dein
CLIENT
Callard & Bowser/USA
AGENCY
Lord Geller Federico Einstein

TOM BODETT: Hi. Tom Bodett for Motel 6 with a few words about roughin' it. Well, when you stay at Motel 6 you'll have to turn the bed down all by yourself, and go without that little piece of chocolate those fancy hotels leave on your pillow. Well, I know it's a lot to ask, but for around 20 bucks, the lowest prices of any national chain, well you can't expect the moon now can you? After all, you do get a clean comfortable room, free TV, movies and local calls. And no service charge on long distance calls. No, we won't bring meals to your room on a silver cart, but that doesn't mean you can't get room service. Since local calls are free, just look up a pizza joint that delivers and give 'em a buzz. They'll bring that large pepperoni pineapple right to your door. So if you can tough it out all in the name of savin' a few bucks, well Motel 6 is where you oughta stay. We've got over 420 locations coast to coast. Just call 505-891-6161 for reservations. I'm Tom Bodett for Motel 6 and we'll leave the light on for you.

1988

WRITERS
David Fowler
Thomas Hripko

AGENCY PRODUCER
Lisa Dee

CLIENT
Motel 6

AGENCY
The Richards Group/Dallas

TOM BODETT: Hi. Tom Bodett for Motel 6 and I'm here to wax a little philosophic. You know at Motel 6 we have a philosophy: people sleep, therefore we are. And the way we figure it, since you don't appreciate artwork when you're sleepin', why hang it in the rooms? I guess if you wanted to be technical though, our walls can be considered art. Abstract art. You know, nothing to get in the way of individual interpretation. Sort of like an empty canvas to be painted on with the mind. Holy smokes, that's deep. I'd just better do the commercial. At Motel 6, you get just what you need. A clean, comfortable room and a good night's sleep for around 22 bucks in most places. a little more in some, and a lot less in others, but always the lowest prices of any national chain and always a heck of a deal. It's a simple philosophy, but it makes good sense. Sort of like a rolling stone not gatherin' any moss. Or that bird in the hand stuff. Ah, I think you get the drift. I'm Tom Bodett, art critic, for Motel 6 and we'll leave the walls bare for you.

1989

WRITER
Thomas Hripko

AGENCY PRODUCER
Lisa Dee

CLIENT
Motel 6

AGENCY
The Richards Group/Dallas

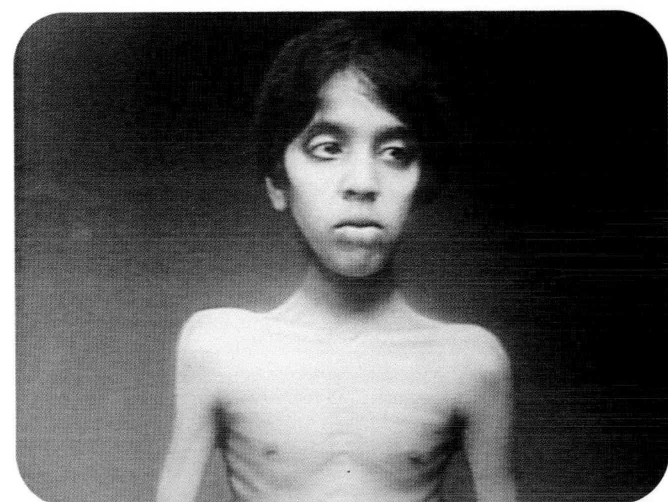

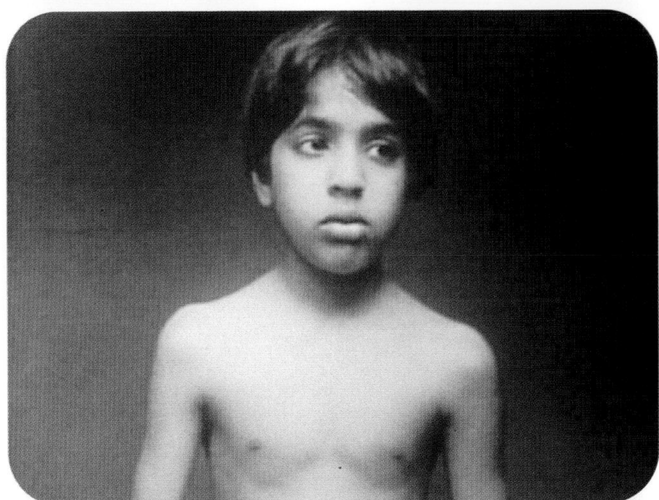

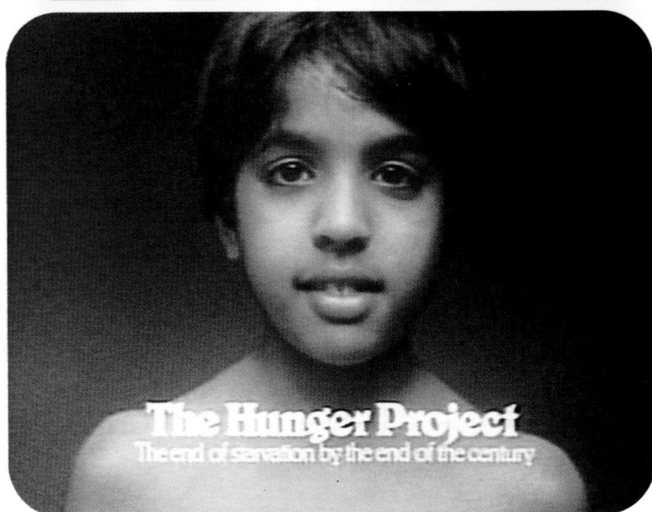

VO: The time has come on our planet for hunger and starvation to end. Not just merely dealt with, not just handled more effectively . . . but to be ended. Finally, once and for all, forever. Starvation will end on this planet by the end of this century. It's an idea whose time has come. The Hunger Project. The end of starvation by the end of the century.

1981

ART DIRECTORS
Ron Travisano
Ron Devito

WRITERS
Ron Travisano
Ron Devito
Neal Rogin

AGENCY PRODUCERS
Dominique Bigar
Peter Yahr

PRODUCTION COMPANY
Nick Samardge

DIRECTOR
Nick Samardge

CLIENT
World Hunger Project

AGENCY
Della Femina Travisano
& Partners

The average cage
in the city animal shelter
isn't much bigger
than this ad.
And that's not the worst of it.
Because after spending five days in a cage like this, many times animals are killed.
And the tragedy is, our city shelters don't have to, or want to, operate like that. Because it's only out of a lack of money, people and space that they're forced to.
At Volunteer Services for Animals, we're working to correct this situation. We're a private, non-profit organization whose sole purpose is to improve the treatment and environment of animals in our state.
But we can't do it all alone. We need people who will help us make shelters better places for animals. We also need people who will participate in fund-raising events. Help find new homes for unclaimed animals. Educate pet owners about animal needs. And, most of all, bring love to the animals.
It really boils down to this. Lost and stray animals in Rhode Island are captured and stuck in cages as if they were criminals.
And the only crime they're really guilty of is being homeless. Call 273-0358 to help.
VOLUNTEER SERVICES ANIMALS
401 Broadway, Providence, Rhode Island 02909

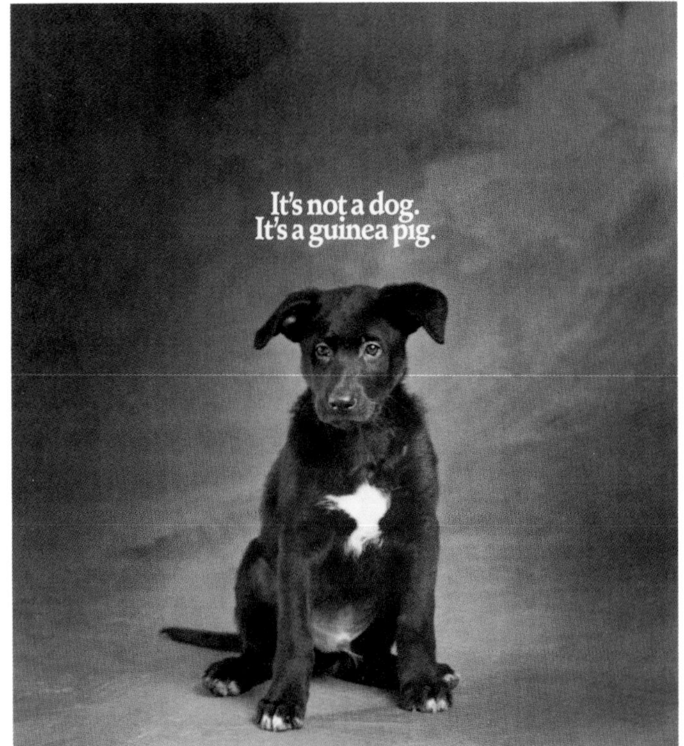

It's not a dog.
It's a guinea pig.

There is a thriving black market in this country. A dreadful, despicable black market.

A black market where lost and stolen pets are sold to laboratories for experimentation.

And while it's true that Rhode Island has passed legislation that makes selling pound animals for experimentation illegal here, it doesn't mean your pet is safe. Because it's a fact that thieves steal pets and smuggle them into states where selling animals for experimentation is legal.

What can you do?

Well, for your own dog, there are three things. One, don't let him run loose in the neighborhood. Keep him on a leash. Two, when you're not home, don't leave him alone in the backyard. And three, if you don't have ID tags, a license or a tattoo on him, get them immediately.

But there's something else you can do. You can join Volunteer Services for Animals.

We're a private, non-profit organization whose sole purpose is to improve the treatment and environment of animals in our state.

We also help municipalities provide humane services which they couldn't otherwise afford. For example, we have lost and found, adoption, veterinary care, population control, pet therapy and education programs.

So please call us at 273-0358.

And help our animal operation prevent animal operations.

401 Broadway, Providence, Rhode Island 02909

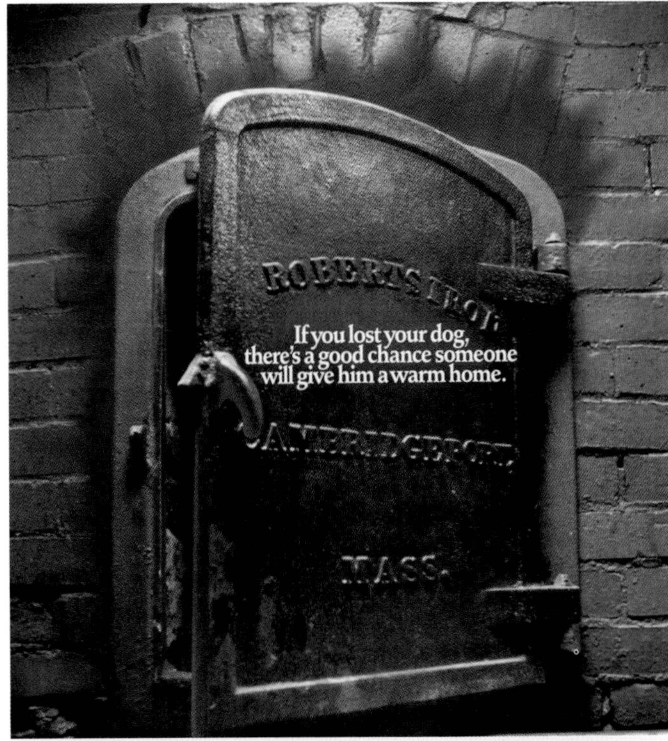

If you lost your dog,
there's a good chance someone
will give him a warm home.
MASS.

What if you had a dog. And what if he wandered away from home and got lost. And what if he was picked up by the city shelter and stuck into a cage.

And what if, what if after five days you still hadn't found him.

You know what would happen? He might be killed. And then cremated in an oven like this. Or buried in the city dump.

Just think how you'd feel. And think how much worse you'd feel knowing city shelters don't have to, or want to, operate like that. Because it's only out of a lack of money, people, and space that they're forced to.

At Volunteer Services for Animals, we're working with Rhode Island municipal shelters to correct this situation.

We're a private, non-profit organization whose sole purpose is to improve the treatment and environment of animals in our state.

We also help municipalities provide humane services which they couldn't otherwise afford. For example, we have lost and found, adoption, veterinary care, population control, pet therapy and education programs.

But we can't do it all alone. We need your help.

We're looking for volunteers who will help us reunite lost pets with their owners. Find new homes for unclaimed animals. Educate pet owners about animal needs. Participate in fundraising events. Help with shelter chores. And, most of all, bring love to the animals.

Look at it this way.

Last year in one Rhode Island city alone, thousands and thousands of lost and stray animals were destroyed. So call us at 273-0358.

Before the subject of unclaimed pets becomes a dead issue.

401 Broadway, Providence, Rhode Island 02909

1985

ART DIRECTORS
Debbie Lucke
Bryan McPeak

WRITER
David Lubars

DESIGNER
Debbie Lucke

ARTISTS
Dom Denardo
Cathleen Toelke

PHOTOGRAPHER
John Holt

CLIENT
Volunteer Services
for Animals

AGENCY
Leonard Monahan Saabye/
Providence, RI

"Before I'll ride with a drunk,
I'll drive myself." –Stevie Wonder
Driving after drinking, or riding with a driver who's been drinking, is a big mistake. Anyone can see that.
This poster of Stevie Wonder should help stop teenagers from killing themselves.
Reader's Digest is putting it in more than 16,000 schools across America—as part of our
challenge to students to devise programs against drinking and driving.
This June the Reader's Digest Foundation will award $500,000 in four year
scholarships to the students who devised the best programs.
To learn more contact your high school principal.

1986

ART DIRECTOR
Bob Barrie

WRITER
Mike Lescarbeau

DESIGNER
Bob Barrie

PHOTOGRAPHER
Bobby Holland

CLIENT
Reader's Digest

AGENCY
Fallon McElligott/
Minneapolis

In the church started by a man who had six wives, forgiveness goes without saying.

The Episcopal Church

1986

ART DIRECTOR
Nancy Rice

WRITER
Tom McElligott

ARTIST
Hans Holbein

CLIENT
Episcopal Church

AGENCY
Fallon McElligott/
Minneapolis

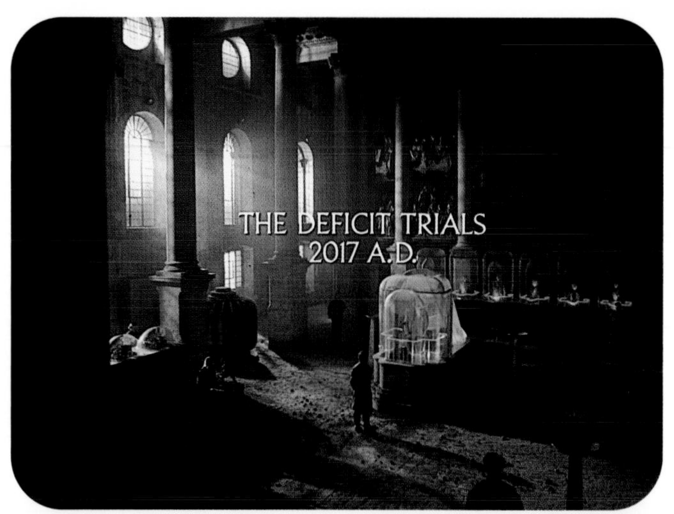

OLD MAN: I've already told you, it was all going to work out somehow. There was even talk of an amendment. But no one was willing to make the sacrifices. I'm afraid you're much too young to understand.

BOY: Maybe so, but I'm afraid the numbers speak for themselves. By 1986, for example, the national debt had reached two trillion dollars. Didn't that frighten you?

VO: No one really knows what another generation of unchecked federal deficits will bring.

OLD MAN: This frightens me.

BOY: No more questions.

OLD MAN: I have a question. Are you ever going to forgive us?

VO: But we know this much. You can change the future. You have to. At W.R. Grace, we want all of us to stay one step ahead of a changing world.

1987

ART DIRECTOR
Steve Ohman

WRITER
Harold Karp

AGENCY PRODUCER
Mindy Gerber

PRODUCTION COMPANIES
Fairbanks Films
RSA Films London

DIRECTOR
Ridley Scott

CLIENT
W. R. Grace & Company

AGENCY
Lowe Marschalk

If you liked pulling the wings off flies as a kid, you may be cut out for a career in animal experimentation.

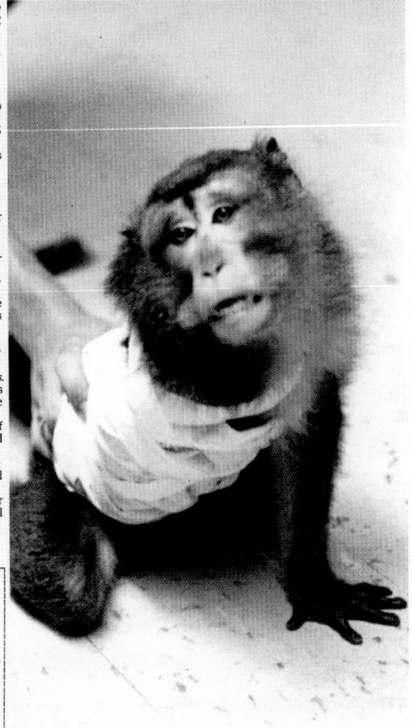

Think of the cruelest thing you can do to an animal and you may qualify for a big government grant.

Think that's an exaggeration? Well, here are just a few of the experiments your tax dollars paid for recently:

Surgically crippled monkeys (one of the monkeys is pictured here) were burned and electro-shocked in a Maryland lab to force them to use their deadened arms.

This experiment cost taxpayers $1.5 million. Until we stopped it.

Conscious, unanaesthetized baboons had their heads locked into a hydraulic device at the University of Pennsylvania. At the flip of a switch, these baboons had their brains scrambled.

This cost U.S. taxpayers $12 million, for almost a dozen years. Until we stopped it.

Immobilized dogs were scheduled to be shot at close range in a Washington, D.C. military test.

It would've cost taxpayers $1.1 million. But we stopped it.

The few atrocities you've read here are just a drop in the bucket of blood that goes by the name "animal research."

Each year, cats, monkeys, dogs, pigs, rats and other lab animals suffer and die by the millions in American laboratories.

The cost to taxpayers is in the *billions*.

If you think these kinds of experiments have no place in the 20th century, please help us stop them.

People for the Ethical Treatment of Animals (PETA) works with medical and legal professionals, the media, members of Congress, and people like you to expose animal abuse and tax waste in the animal experimentation industry.

We've brought an end to many horror stories, but there are thousands of other cruel experiments being conducted even as you read this ad.

So please join us today.

Yes, I want to help stop the abuse of animals in experiments.

Name ______

Address ______

City ______ State ______ Zip ______

Please accept my tax-deductible contribution of: $15 ______

$25 ______ $50 ______ $100 ______ other ______

Contributors of $15 or more receive a free copy of the book *Animal Liberation*.

People For The Ethical Treatment Of Animals

P.O. Box 42516 Washington, D.C. 20015 (202) 726-0156

Thanks to a $12 million government grant, scientists have conclusive proof that monkeys die when their skulls are crushed.

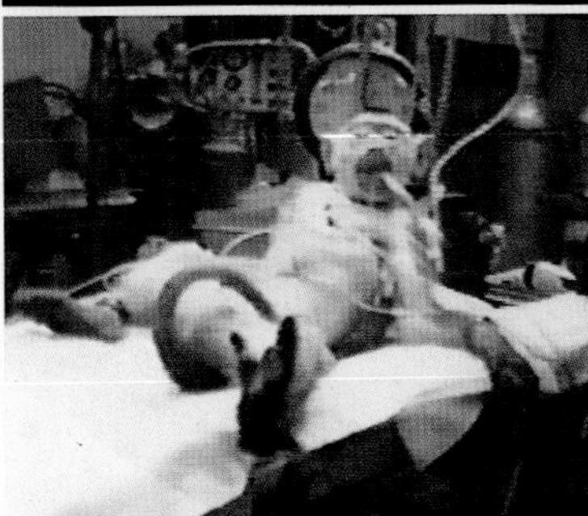

Did you know what other "experiments" that you've helped underwrite with your hard-earned tax dollars?

You paid to have a group of grown men keep a group of cats awake for a week straight.

Cats that were then placed on floating pieces of wood to see how long the cats' fear of falling in would keep them awake. Proving exactly what? Anything?

Care for another? To test the effectiveness of the Heimlich maneuver (already well-documented as effective), another federally-funded lab wanted to drown some dogs.

Fortunately, the scientists were drowned with letters instead (thanks to an effort by our organization) and the experiment was called off.

That experiment isn't the only one we've managed to have had scrapped.

We helped raise such an outroar over the head-injury research on the monkeys you see in these pictures, that it was closed down.

But for every sadistic and scientifically worthless experiment we've shut down, there are literally thousands we haven't.

People For The Ethical Treatment Of Animals (PETA) works with medical and legal professionals, the media, members of Congress, and people like you to help expose animal abuse and tax waste in this horrible animal experimentation industry.

We've brought an end to many horror stories, but thousands of cruel experiments are being conducted even as you read this ad.

That's why we're asking for your help. Because our opponents don't listen to moral arguments or pleas of mercy.

They have to be pinned down in court.

So please, send us your tax-deductible contribution today. And thank you.

Yes, I want to help stop the abuse of animals in experiments.

Name ______

Address ______

City ______ State ______ Zip ______

Please accept my tax-deductible contribution of: $15 ______

$25 ______ $50 ______ $100 ______ other ______

Contributors of $15 or more receive a free copy of the book *Animal Liberation*.

People For The Ethical Treatment Of Animals

Imagine having your body left to science while you're still in it.

Three animals die every second in U.S. laboratories.

The monkey pictured here was surgically crippled and then forced to use his deadened arm.

Other animals, including rabbits, dogs, and cats are routinely blinded, shocked, mutilated, decapitated and force-fed poisons in tests which could easily be replaced with modern and more reliable alternative tests.

These sadistic animal tests are being conducted by the government, universities, medical associations, and profit-making corporations.

And always behind closed, locked doors. Pigs, rats, chickens, horses and other laboratory animals suffer by the millions.

The cost to U.S. taxpayers, however, is in the billions.

If you think these kinds of cruel experiments have no place in the 20th century, please join us: People for the Ethical Treatment of Animals.

PETA is America's leading animal rights organization. By working with medical and legal professionals, the media, members of Congress, and people like you, PETA has been able to stop some of the most horrifying animal experiments, including the one pictured here.

Even as you read this ad, there are thousands more lab experiments being conducted without your knowledge, *but with your tax dollars.*

So please join us today.

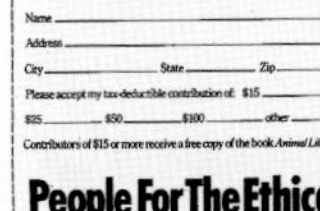

Yes, I want to help stop the abuse of animals in experiments.

Name ______

Address ______

City ______ State ______ Zip ______

Please accept my tax-deductible contribution of: $15 ______

$25 ______ $50 ______ $100 ______ other ______

Contributors of $15 or more receive a free copy of the book *Animal Liberation*.

People For The Ethical Treatment Of Animals

P.O. Box 42516 Washington, D.C. 20015 (202) 726-0156

1988

ART DIRECTOR
Wayne Gibson

WRITER
Luke Sullivan

CLIENT
People for the Ethical Treatment of Animals

AGENCY
The Martin Agency/
Richmond, VA

LET US NOT FORGET THAT 4,200 AMERICANS DIED HERE TO BUILD A NATION, NOT A PARKING LOT.

One hot July afternoon in 1861, the first major battle of the Civil War took place. A Union force of 30,000 men, the Army of the Potomac, sought to end the rebellious Southern secession.

The battle was to take place near a creek bed called Bull Run in Manassas, Virginia. There a slightly larger Confederate Army under General Thomas Jackson set up its defenses.

Onlookers with picnic baskets watched, expecting the Union Soldiers to make short work of the Southern force. What they saw was a Confederate General stand so firmly against wave after wave of Union assaults, that he earned the nickname "Stonewall."

Then they watched as a Confederate counterattack sent the Army of the Potomac back to the Potomac.

Thirteen months after, General Robert E. Lee routed another Union Army at Bull Run ending the North's hope of a quick end to the war.

Now a real estate developer wants to transform much of this 542 acre tract of trees, hills and lush wetlands into a shopping mall. He wants to build an office complex and add 560 residential houses.

And if you don't think traffic into Washington is crowded enough now, just imagine what this "Williams Center" will bring. What's worse? Most of that traffic will come through the remains of this historic park.

Is a shopping mall how we pay tribute to almost 29,000 casualties? Many of those who died here were barely more than boys. They gave their lives trying to do what they thought was right. Thousands of them died unidentified and were piled into mass graves, their names and histories to be forever forgotten.

If Manassas battlefield is transformed into a shopping mall, then is any part of our national heritage safe from real estate moguls and avaricious county tax commissioners?

We have to stop the county from allowing these developers to desecrate what amounts to nothing less than a national historic monument. What is at stake is more than just the memories of what happened here. What is at stake are our values.

Are frozen yogurt, plastic watches and prewashed jeans more important than a piece of our history?

Please send us your contributions. Give us your phone number if you can volunteer. And definitely call or write your congressman and senator and tell them how you feel.

Let us not allow the 4,200 Americans who died here to be paved over.

SAVE THE BATTLEFIELD COALITION.

Save The Battlefield Coalition, P.O. Box 110, Catharpin, Virginia 22018
Engravings and posters donated by Graphics 3 engravers, Richmond, Virginia (804) 788-4333.

MAY THEIR SOULS REST IN PEACE. NOT IN A SHOPPING MALL.

Is a shopping mall and office complex a proper tribute to the men who paid the ultimate price for their country? Is the potential tax revenue worth paving over an irreplaceable piece of our national heritage? Can nothing stop developer John T. Hazel from razing Manassas Battlefield?

Consider that over 4,000 men died at Manassas, some in horrible agony. Consider that some 18,000 men were maimed here. Over 5,000 disappeared in enfilading gunfire and were piled into mass graves, their names and histories to be forever forgotten.

Consider that many of the men who died here were barely more than boys trying to do their patriotic duty.

It was on this place that two famous Civil War battles occurred. In July of 1861, a Union General named McDowell led a force, 30,000 strong, against a similar Confederate force along the creek bed named Bull Run.

Confederate forces, under General Thomas Jackson stood their ground against wave after bloody wave of Union troops. It was here that "Stonewall" Jackson earned his nickname.

Thirteen months later, at the Second Battle of Bull Run, General Robert E. Lee routed another Union army, ending any chance for a quick victory. The casualties from this skirmish were staggering.

Right now there are plans to desecrate these most hallowed grounds with parking lots, frozen yogurt and pre-washed jeans.

We have to stop John T. Hazel from making a vulgar mockery of this place where so many gave their lives to build a country, not a parking lot.

Please send what you can to the Save The Battlefield Coalition. Let us not allow the deaths of 4,200 men to be in vain.

SAVE THE BATTLEFIELD COALITION.

Save The Battlefield Coalition, P.O. Box 110, Catharpin, Virginia 22018
Engravings and posters donated by Graphics 3 engravers, Richmond, Virginia (804) 788-4333.

IF WE PAY TRIBUTE TO THE 4,200 SOLDIERS WHO DIED AT MANASSAS WITH VIDEOS, FROZEN YOGURT AND PREWASHED JEANS, THEN WE'RE THE ONES WHO ARE DEAD.

Take your children to the park that was once Manassas Battlefield. Do it soon. Walk them through this 542 acre tract.

Take them there and tell them the story of how two great battles were fought on this land not long ago.

Show your children where "Stonewall" Jackson earned his nickname. Show them the creek bed named Bull Run, where mass graves were dug to cover thousands of nameless soon-to-be-forgotten soldiers.

Soldiers who spilled their blood on this place to preserve a nation.

Do this tonight, if you can. Sit there for a while and enjoy the peace.

Listen to the birds. Smell the wildflowers.

Then pray that your children will remember this time and this place. Because soon it won't be here anymore.

Soon, the only thing you'll hear is the endless rushing of cars and trucks as they pile in and out of the Williams Center.

Soon, the only thing you'll smell are fumes as commuters jockey for parking spaces.

Soon, the only thing you'll see are retail outlets and glass and brick buildings.

In July of 1861, the first major battle of the Civil War took place on these grounds. Union General McDowell led a force of 30,000 men against a slightly larger Confederate Army.

It was his and Lincoln's hope that this would be the end of the Southern insurrection.

Onlookers from high vantage points set picnics to watch the Union triumph. They watched as wave after wave of troops attacked Confederate General Thomas Jackson.

They watched as he held his ground and earned the nickname "Stonewall."

But they fled when Jackson counterattacked and forced Union troops all the way back to Washington.

Thirteen months later, another battle took place at Bull Run. This time General Robert E. Lee led the Confederate Army in what was, perhaps, his greatest military victory.

For three days men clashed, men who were hardly more than boys. They fought until they had no more ammunition. Then they fought with rocks and knives.

Many of the second battle's casualties were piled into mass graves, their identities unknown.

The wounded died in horrible agony while awaiting what meager medical attention was available to them.

Thanks to a real estate developer, yet another battle rages at Manassas today, a multimillionaire real estate developer has already razed important parts of the park to build a 1.2 million square foot shopping mall, a 1.7 million square foot office park and some 560 residential homes and townhomes.

Practically overnight, this historic, tranquil tract of land is being transformed into another symbol of consumerism. Sure, we need the revenue.

But what price will the county tax commissioner put on the blood of almost 29,000 men? If Manassas Battlefield becomes a shopping mall, what's next?

Perhaps Arlington National Cemetery will make a good theme park. Is any part of our national heritage safe from developers?

What is at stake here is our very sense of values. It's one thing to learn about our past from a textbook. It's quite something else to see it. To feel it. To smell it. To touch it. To preserve it. To remember our past so that, perhaps, we will not repeat it.

We need your help. We need your contributions to save one of the last beautiful D.C. suburbs from "progress."

We need you to help us stop developers from desecrating what amounts to nothing less than a national historic monument.

Please send your funds to the Save The Battlefield Coalition. Give us what you can. Give us your phone number if you can volunteer time. Write your congressmen and your senators and tell them how you feel.

Let us not allow the thousands who died here to have died in vain.

Save the battlefield from development. From shopping malls and office complexes.
Enclosed is my contribution of $ ____________

Name ____________

Address ____________

City ____________ State ______ Zip ______

Phone ____________

SAVE THE BATTLEFIELD COALITION.

Send to Save The Battlefield Coalition, P.O. Box 110, Catharpin, Virginia 22018
Engravings and posters donated by Graphics 3 engravers, Richmond, Virginia (804) 788-4333.

1989

ART DIRECTOR
Wayne Gibson

WRITER
Daniel Clay Russ

CLIENT
Save The Battlefield Coalition

AGENCY
The Martin Agency/
Richmond, VA

Original. Chunky.

When we make Prince Spaghetti Sauce, we give you a choice. Because no two people have quite the same taste. PRINCE

1986

ART DIRECTOR
Bob Barrie

WRITER
John Stingley

DESIGNER
Bob Barrie

ARTISTS
Dick Hess
Mark Hess

CLIENT
Prince Spaghetti Sauce

AGENCY
Fallon McElligott/
Minneapolis

1984

ART DIRECTOR
Gary Johns

WRITER
Jeff Gorman

PHOTOGRAPHER
Carl Furuta

CLIENT
Nike

AGENCY
Chiat/Day - Los Angeles

Let us finance your midlife crisis.

Talk to us about Auto Financing today. Call 1-800-621-3817.

Continental Illinois
We work hard. We have to.

An Equal Opportunity Lender. © 1986 Continental Illinois National Bank and Trust Company of Chicago.

1987

ART DIRECTOR
Bob Barrie

WRITER
Mike Lescarbeau

PHOTOGRAPHER
Steve Umland

CLIENT
Continental Illinois

AGENCY
Fallon McElligott/
Minneapolis

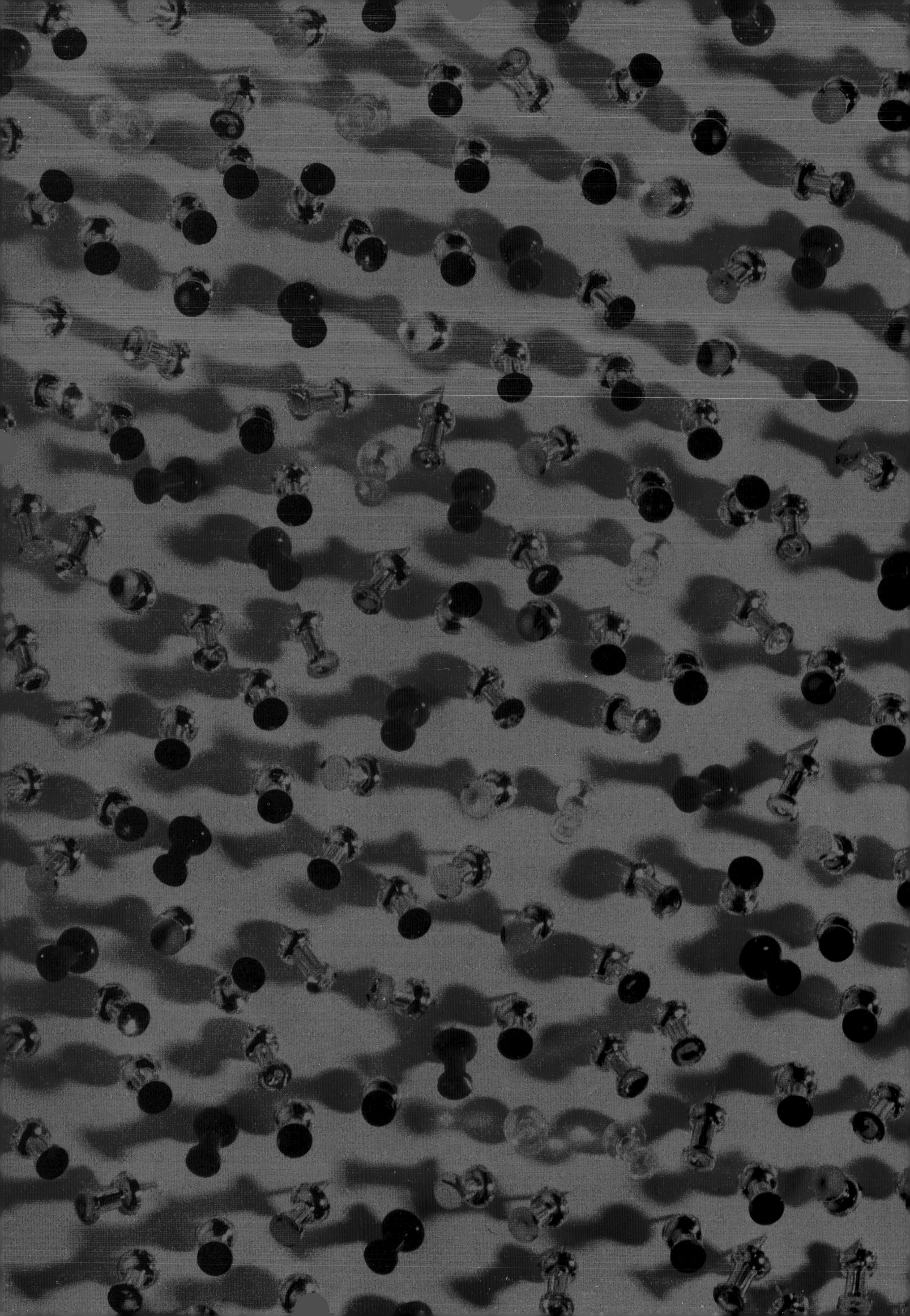